GW00587825

跟我学汉语
第二版

LEARN CHINESE WITH ME

学生用书 3

Student's Book 3

人民教育出版社

PEOPLE'S EDUCATION PRESS

·北京·

图书在版编目（CIP）数据

跟我学汉语学生用书 ：第 2 版 ：英语版．第 3 册 /
陈绂等编．— 北京 ：人民教育出版社，2015.3
ISBN 978-7-107-29702-1

Ⅰ．①跟… Ⅱ．①陈… Ⅲ．①汉语－对外汉语教学－
教材 Ⅳ．①H195.4

中国版本图书馆 CIP 数据核字（2015）第 068868 号

人民教育出版社 出版发行
网址：http://www.pep.com.cn
北京盛通印刷股份有限公司印装　全国新华书店经销
2015 年 3 月第 1 版　2017 年 1 月第 2 次印刷
开本：890 毫米 ×1 240 毫米　1/16　插页：1　印张：15.5　印数：3 001～6 000册
审图号：GS（2014）5232 号
定价：84.00 元

如发现印、装质量问题，影响阅读，请与本社出版部联系调换。
（联系地址：北京市海淀区中关村南大街 17 号院 1 号楼　邮编：100081）
电话：010-58759215　电子邮箱：yzzlfk@pep.com.cn
Printed in the People's Republic of China

总 策 划　　许　琳　　殷忠民　　韦志榕

总 监 制　　夏建辉　　郑旺全

监 　 制　　张彤辉　　刘根芹　　王世友　　赵晓非

编 　 者　　陈　绂　　朱志平　　王若江　　宋志明

　　　　　　杨丽姣　　尹　洁　　徐彩华　　娄　毅

英文翻译　　李长英　　胡　凝

责任编辑　　狄国伟

审 　 稿　　赵晓非　　王世友

英文审稿　　Meredith Chester [美国]

封面设计　　王俊宏

插图制作　　北京天辰文化艺术传播有限公司

　　　　　　北京碧悠动漫文化有限公司

第二版前言

《跟我学汉语》的出版和使用已经整整十年了。十年间，它受到国外汉语学习者的普遍欢迎，对此，我们由衷地感到欣慰。目前汉语作为第二语言的教学正在飞速地发展，学习汉语的人群，特别是海外学习汉语的人数迅速增加，为了使教材能更好地为汉语国际传播的大好形势服务，在国家汉办的领导下，在人民教育出版社的协助下，我们对《跟我学汉语》进行了全面的修订。

参加这次修订的人员，有的是第一版教材的编写者，有的是美国AP中文教材的编写者。作为从事并热爱汉语教学的教师，我们认真研究了使用这套教材的教师们和海外其他从事汉语为第二语言教学工作的一线教师们的意见，参考了《新汉语水平考试（HSK）大纲》《国际汉语教学通用课程大纲》及相关国家的汉语课程标准，并结合自己多年的教学实践，对《跟我学汉语》的修订确定了如下原则与方法：

首先，基本保持第一版教材编写的指导思想、框架与风格，适用对象仍然是以零为起点，终点达到中级汉语水平的学习者。完成全部四册学习后能掌握1 500个词以上，达到HSK四级的水平。

其次，更加明确了"学习外语的根本目的就是为了完成交际任务"这一外语学习理念，并将这一理念体现在教材的每个组成部分之中，尤其是课堂设计和练习的编写中。

第三，在修订中始终致力于增强教材的普适性和针对性。第一版教材主要针对北美地区，修订后的第二版教材将适用于海外大部分地区。不少一线教师提出，《跟我学汉语》是一部高中教材，但部分内容显得有些低龄化，修订中我们注意认真纠正这一倾向，力争使教材更加适用于海外的高中学生。

第四，适度削减教材的内容，将每一册的教学总量压缩了20%左右；为了降低教材的难度，重新安排了部分课文和语言点，以更符合《国际汉语教学通用课程大纲》和HSK的要求；为了增加教材的趣味性，重新设计了课堂活动和部分练习题……其他诸如关于拼音的说明与教学、关于汉字教学、词语教学以及文化内容的介绍等等，我们都做了适度的调整与补充。

第五，适量补充新内容。在适度削减的总原则下，为了帮助海外汉语教师备课，我们对第一版教材做了一定的补充：在学生用书中用英语给出了有关语言点的最简单的说明，以便学生了解和学习；同时在教师用书中又做了较为详细的解释与扩展，为教师备课提供了可用的资料。我们还较大篇幅地增加了教师用书的内容，在"教学建议"栏目中增设了"教学安排"，给出了具体的"教学程序"。为了更好地与HSK衔接，我们在教师用书中增加了HSK模拟试题，帮助学生熟悉题型，同时有针对性地进行自我评测。

由于本次修订的时间比较紧，第二版内容中可能还会有各种问题，我们诚恳希望广大使用者能够给予批评指正。

本次修订得到了孔子学院总部的直接指导和人民教育出版社的大力支持，在此表示衷心的感谢！我们还特别要向给本教材提出宝贵意见的教师致以最诚挚的谢意！

编　者

2014年11月

Preface
(to the Second Edition)

Learn Chinese with Me has now been in publication for over ten years, during which time we have been very pleased to note its warm reception in the Chinese learning community. However, during that time, the field of teaching Chinese as a second language has developed at a rapid rate. Concurrently, more and more students are choosing to study Chinese as a second language every year. To better serve the needs of our students and ensure that our teaching materials incorporate these recent developments, Hanban and the People's Education Press have come together to create a second edition of *Learn Chinese with Me*.

Editors of this edition include both editors of the first edition and AP Chinese instructors in the United States. As teachers with a passionate commitment to the study and teaching of Chinese, we have taken into careful consideration the suggestions of Chinese teachers that have used this textbook series, as well as those of teachers in related fields, consulted the *New HSK Outline*, the *International Curriculum for Chinese Language Education* and other relevant curriculum standards, and combined them with our own years of experience to decide on the following five principles in performing our revisions of *Learn Chinese with Me*:

First, maintaining the guiding principles, framework and style of the first edition, we have made this series suitable for students with no prior Chinese learning experience. By the time students complete the series, their Chinese will be approaching the intermediate level. After completing all four volumes, they will qualify for HSK Level Four.

Second, we have more explicitly incorporated the concept that "the study of a foreign language's ultimate goal is to be able to complete tasks" into every section of the teaching materials, especially in the compilation of in-the-classroom plans and practice exercises.

Third, throughout the entire revision process, we have attempted to make the series more generalizable to students of Chinese all around the world, as well as more suitable for our target demographic of high school students. While the original edition was mainly directed at students in North America, this edition aims to suit students from many different world regions. Additionally, many teachers advised us that, while the first edition of *Learn Chinese with Me* was a high school series, part of the content was more suited to younger students. We have industriously worked to address this tendency in the current edition and make the content more suitable for high school students outside of China.

Fourth, we have decreased the content to more moderate levels, compressing each volume by about 20%. To decrease the difficulty of the material and better suit the requirements of both the *International Curriculum for Chinese Language Education* and the HSK, we have adjusted text and added grammar sections. To make the material more interesting, we have designed new classroom activities and group practice assignments. We have also revised and supplemented existing sections, such as the explanation and teaching of *pinyin*, the teaching of Chinese characters and vocabulary, and the introduction of certain aspects of Chinese culture.

Fifth, we have added a moderate amount of new material. While keeping our goal of decreasing content in mind, we have supplemented certain sections to help teachers prepare lessons. As many teachers mentioned that the first edition lacked adequate explanations of grammar patterns, the revised student edition of *Learn Chinese with Me* includes simple English introductions to new grammar patterns in order to help students understand them more easily. Additionally, the revised teacher's book once more includes more detailed and developed explanations as well as class preparation materials. We have also increased the length of the content in the teacher's book. Under the heading "Teaching Suggestions," we have designed "Teaching Schedules", as well as provided a model "Teaching Sequence" for teaching the course. In order to better match the format of the HSK, from the first volume's second unit onward, we have added a practice set of HSK questions in the Teacher's book. These will help students become familiar with the HSK question format and allow them to review how far they have progressed.

Due to the relatively short timeframe given for revision, this edition may contain some errors, so we sincerely welcome any critique or corrections from users of the series.

We would like to express our wholehearted thanks for Confucius Institute Headquarters' direct guidance and the People's Education Press' great support in revising this series. We would also like to extend our sincere gratitude toward the many teachers that provided valuable suggestions throughout the editing process!

Compilers

November, 2014

第一版前言

　　《跟我学汉语》是一套专为海外中学生编写的汉语教材，使用对象主要是以英语为母语的中学生或者年龄在15—18岁的青少年第二语言学习者。

　　《跟我学汉语》凝聚了我们这些从事并热爱汉语教学的教师们的大量心血。这套教材从框架的设计到语言材料的选取安排，都吸收了当前汉语作为第二语言习得研究、特别是对以英语为母语的汉语习得研究的最新成果。由于编写者都是汉语作为第二语言教学的教师，因此能够从自己亲身进行教学的角度去设计教材，安排内容。在编写的过程中，我们也多次征求并采纳了海外中学以汉语为第二语言进行教学的一线教师的意见，这些意见给予了编写工作很好的启示。

　　《跟我学汉语》这套教材以零为起点，终点接近中级汉语水平。编写的主导思想是培养海外中学生学习汉语的兴趣。教材在内容的安排上力图自然、有趣，符合第二语言学习规律。教材语法点的出现顺序以表达功能的需要为基础，并用话题为线索来编排语言材料，从而带动交际能力的培养。《跟我学汉语》采用的话题得益于海外广大中学生的热情贡献。2001年编者在北美地区对两个城市的中学生进行了"你感兴趣的话题"的问卷调查，这套教材的话题即是从500多份调查材料中精心筛选出来的。我们希望，这套教材能够在不失系统性的基础上，表现出明显的功能性；在不失科学性的基础上，表现出明显的实用性；在不失严肃性的基础上，表现出明显的趣味性。

　　《跟我学汉语》全套教材共12册，包括学生用书4册以及配套的教师用书、练习册各4册，同时有与学生用书相配套的语音听力材料和多媒体教材。全套教材可供英语地区中学汉语教学9—12年级使用。

《跟我学汉语》是中国国家对外汉语教学领导小组办公室（简称国家汉办）所主持的一项重点研究项目的一部分，由北京师范大学承担。在编写这套教材的过程中，我们得到了方方面面的支持与帮助。为此，我们衷心感谢：

国家汉办严美华主任、姜明宝副主任、李桂苓女士、宋永波先生，他们的具体指导给予了教材编写最为有力的帮助；

加拿大温哥华、多伦多地区的汉语教师：Jean Heath, Kate McMeiken, Tina Du, Chong Fu Tan, Hua Tang, Larry Zehong Lei, Assunta Tan A.M., Maggie Ip, Billie Ng, Yanfeng Qu, Hilary Spicer, Tina Ding, Xue Wu, 王献恩、李建一、高锡铭、戴大器、宋乃王……他们在教材的前期调研中提供了大量的帮助，在他们的帮助下，我们走近了北美地区，走近了我们要编写的教材；

美国芝加哥地区的汉语教师：纪瑾、车幼鸣、谢洪伟、李迪、傅海燕、顾利程，他们认真地试用了教材的初稿，并提出了宝贵的意见；

中国驻加拿大温哥华总领事馆教育参赞许琳女士、中国驻加拿大多伦多总领事馆教育参赞张国庆先生，他们以及他们的同事为教材的前期调研提供了大量帮助，为教材的编写付出了许多心血和精力，他们的热情和坦诚都令人感动；

中国驻美国芝加哥总领事馆教育组的江波、朱宏清等先生，他们为这套教材的试用与修改做了许多工作；

国家汉办原常务副主任、北京语言学院副院长程棠先生认真地审阅了全部学生用书、教师用书和练习册，并提出了中肯的意见。

在教材编写的初期和后期，国家汉办先后两次组织专家对教材的样课和定稿进行了审定，专家们提出了许多宝贵意见，我们在此一并致谢。

编　者

2003年6月

Preface
(to the First Edition)

Learn Chinese with Me is a series of textbooks designed especially for overseas high school students. It is mainly targeted at students of Chinese language, aged between 15 and 18 years old, whose native language is English.

Learn Chinese with Me is a product of many years' painstaking labor carried out with a passion and devotion to the cause of Chinese teaching. During the process of compiling this series (from the framework design to the selection and arrangement of the language materials), we have taken into consideration the latest research on the acquisition of Chinese as a second language, especially on the acquisition of Chinese by English-speakers, our own experiences of teaching Chinese as a second language and feedback from numerous other Chinese language teachers working on the front line. We were able to design the textbooks and arrange the content on the basis of a wide spectrum of knowledge and experience, both academic and practical.

This series of textbooks guides the students from beginner to low-intermediate level. The compiling principle is to foster high school students' interest in learning Chinese. The content is natural and interesting and arranged in accordance with the rules of learning a second language. To cope with the general needs of conducting daily communication, the sentence patterns and grammar are presented to students in an order that emphasizes functional usage and the language materials are arranged within situational topics. The selection of these topics owes a great deal to overseas high school students themselves. In 2001, we conducted a survey among high school students in two North American cities on *Topics That You're Interested in*, and the topics in this series of textbooks have been carefully selected based on this survey of over 500 questionnaires. It is our goal that this textbook series is, on the one hand, functional, pragmatic and interesting to the learner, and on the other hand, systematic, scientific, and academic.

The entire series of *Learn Chinese with Me* is composed of 12 books, including 4 Student's Books, 4 Teacher's Books, 4 Workbooks and other phonetic and listening materials and multimedia materials supplemented to the Student's Books. The series can meet the needs of teaching Chinese to 9-12 grades in English-speaking countries and communities.

This series of textbooks is part of a major project sponsored by China National Office for Teaching Chinese as a Foreign Language (NOCFL) and entrusted to Beijing Normal University to carry out. During the whole compiling process, we received assistance and support from various parties. Therefore, we'd like to dedicate our gratitude to:

Yan Meihua, Director of NOCFL, Jiang Mingbao, Vice Director of NOCFL, Ms. Li Guiling and Mr. Song Yongbo. Their specific directions have been of crucial assistance to us.

We would also like to thank the teachers in Vancouver and Toronto, Canada. They are Jean Heath, Kate McMeiken, Tina Du, Chong Fu Tan, Hua Tang, Larry Zehong Lei, Assunta Tan A.M., Maggie Ip, Billie Ng, Yanfeng Qu, Hilary Spicer, Tina Ding, Xue Wu, Xian'en Wang, Jianyi Lee, Ximing Gao, Daqi Dai and Naiwang Song etc. Through their help in the area of research and their valuable suggestions, we acquired a better knowledge of the North American classroom and finally came closer than ever before to the kind of textbook we have always strived to create.

The teachers of Chinese in Chicago, Jin Ji, Youming Che, Hongwei Xie, Di Lee, Haiyan Fu and Licheng Gu also provided valuable suggestions after they carefully read the first draft of the textbook.

We also really appreciate the great assistance offered by Ms. Xu Lin, Educational Attaché of the General Chinese Consulate in Vancouver, Canada and Mr. Zhang Guoqing, Educational Attaché of the General Chinese Consulate in Toronto, Canada. They and their colleagues gave us lots of help during our long-time survey for this book. Their devotion, enthusiasm and sincerity for the project has deeply impressed us.

Mr. Jiang Bo and Mr. Zhu Hongqing in charge of education in General Chinese Consulate in Chicago also made many contributions to the trial use and revision of this series.

In addition, we would like to give our special thanks to Mr. Cheng Tang, the former Vice Director of the Standing Committee of NOCFL and the Vice President of Beijing Language Institute. He made many critical proposals to us based on his careful study of all the Student's Books, the Teacher's Books and the Workbooks, and offered some invaluable suggestions.

At both the beginning and late stages of compiling this textbook series, NOCFL twice organized experts to examine and evaluate the textbook sample and the final draft. These experts, too, provided useful comments on the series. We are also grateful to them.

Compilers
June, 2003

A Map of China's Administrative Regions

Types of Facial Makeup in Peking Operas

Peking opera, Chinese traditional opera, is loved by many people not only because of its attractive vocal music and acrobatic fighting but also because of its rich and fine facial make-up. The style of the makeup is based on the character's personality and characteristics. The various types of makeup in Peking opera represent different Chinese historic or legendary figures. The following facial makeup represent some well-known Chinese historic and legendary figures, who later became famous characters in Peking opera.

Can you guess who they are? You may find out the answers by asking Chinese people around you to tell you the stories about them. You can tell these stories to your classmates.

Work together with your classmates to try to paint some facial makeup by yourselves!

Cao Cao

Baogong

Zhong Kui

Sun Wukong

Methods and Steps of Facial Makeup

(1) Make a mask. Make a mud face model according to the shape and size of an actual person's face.

(2) Draw an opera mask. On a piece of white paper draw a mask that is of the same size and shape as the one you have made. As most Peking opera masks are symmetrical, you should first draw a vertical line down through the middle and then draw the half of the facial feature on one side. Copy the half you have drawn on to the opposite side. The next step is to add the color.

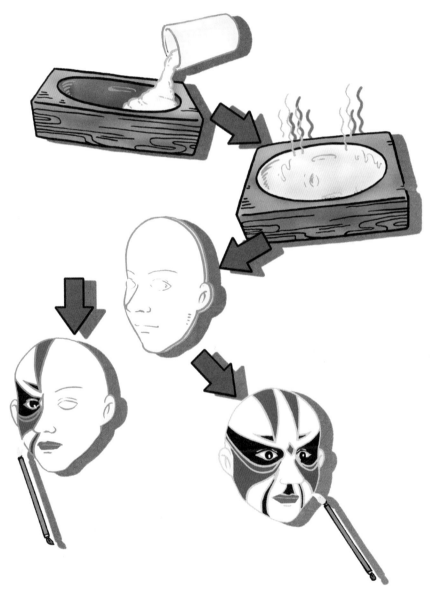

CONTENTS

Unit Three   *Two Generations*   68

Unit Four   *Different Cultures*   102

Table of Combinations of Initials and Finals in *Putonghua*

Unit One

Meiyun's Family

1 她从香港来

Getting started

What's your home like? Describe the layout of the home according to the given pictures.

现房出租 (xiànfáng chūzū)

两层楼房 (liǎng céng lóufáng)，三个卧室 (wòshì) 在楼上 (lóu shang)，客厅 (kètīng) 和厨房 (chúfáng) 在楼下 (lóu xià)，院子 (yuànzi) 里有车库 (chēkù)。1800元/月。如果您感兴趣，请打电话：433-8257; 982-6768。

For Rent

Text 1

Jack, Ma Ming's old pal, comes to visit Ma Ming.

马明：杰克，好久(hǎojiǔ)不见(jiàn)了！ ①

杰克：你好，马明，好久不见！

马明：暑假过得(de)怎么样？

杰克：过得不错。你呢，最近忙不忙？

马明：很忙。我在帮我的邻居搬(bān)家。

杰克：帮你的邻居搬家？

马明：是啊，我爸爸的朋友从香港(Xiānggǎng)来，现在是我们家
　　　的邻居。

Meiyun walks out of her home.

杰克：那个女孩儿(nǚháir)是谁？

马明：她就是我邻居的女儿(nǚ'ér)。

杰克：她长得很漂亮。

马明：她姓李(Lǐ)，叫美云(Měiyún)。来，我给你介绍一下……

---

① 好久不见了：Long time no see!

Text 2

Ma Ming is introducing Meiyun's family.

李先生是我爸爸的朋友。他们一家从香港来，现在是我们的邻居。李先生今年42岁，他高(gāo)高的，瘦瘦的，戴着(zhe)一副眼镜(yǎnjìng)①。他的太太(tàitai)矮(ǎi)矮的，胖(pàng)胖的，经常笑眯眯(xiàomīmī)的。他们的女儿叫美云，长得很漂亮，今年16岁，现在是我的同学。李先生还有个儿子(érzi)叫美华(Měihuá)，今年9岁。他长得很可爱(kě'ài)，有一张圆(yuán)圆的脸(liǎn)②，一双大大的眼睛(yǎnjing)。

---

① 戴着一副眼镜：wearing a pair of glasses
② 有一张圆圆的脸：with chubby cheeks (literal: a round face)

New words

1.	好久	hǎojiǔ	*adj.*	long time
2.	见	jiàn	*v.*	to see
3.	得	de	*pt.*	*used to link a verb or an adjective to a complement which describes the manner or degree*
4.	搬	bān	*v.*	to move (house)
5.	女孩儿	nǚháir	*n.*	girl
6.	女儿	nǚ'ér	*n.*	daughter
7.	高	gāo	*adj.*	tall
8.	着	zhe	*pt.*	*added to a verb or an adjective to indicate a continued action or state*
9.	眼镜	yǎnjìng	*n.*	glasses
10.	太太	tàitai	*n.*	Mrs
11.	矮	ǎi	*adj.*	short (of stature)
12.	胖	pàng	*adj.*	fat
13.	笑眯眯	xiàomīmī	*adj.*	smiling
14.	儿子	érzi	*n.*	son
15.	可爱	kě'ài	*adj.*	cute; lovely
16.	圆	yuán	*adj.*	round; chubby
17.	脸	liǎn	*n.*	face
18.	眼睛	yǎnjing	*n.*	eye

Proper nouns

1.	香港	Xiānggǎng	Hong Kong
2.	李	Lǐ	Li
3.	美云	Měiyún	Meiyun
4.	美华	Měihuá	Meihua

1. "她就是我邻居的女儿。"

   就 is an adverb. Put before the verb 是 in this sentence, 就 plays a role of strengthening and affirming.

   这就是我们的学校。

   我们就是这里的住户。

2. "她长得很漂亮。"

   In this sentence, 长 is the verb, while 很漂亮 is its complement indicating the state and degree of 长 , with 很 indicating degree. 得 plays a connecting role between the verb and complement.

   他跑得很快。

   我高兴得很。

3. "他高高的，瘦瘦的，戴着一副眼镜。"

   Both 高 and 瘦 are mono-syllable adjectives which are repeated here to make the description more vivid and lively.

   他的个子高高的。

   妈妈有一张圆圆的脸。

Exercise

On your own

Rearrange the following words and phrases according to the texts and then write their numbers in the pheonix's tail to make a complete sentence.

(1) 马明①　　他的邻居②　　帮③　　搬家④

(2) 就是①　　我②　　妈妈③　　的④　　她⑤

(3) 长得①　　很②　　李美云③　　漂亮④

Conversation practice

1. Choose a response in the bubble that can best complete each of the following conversations and
then practice in pairs.

①

2. In pairs, practice greeting friends. Write the differences between greeting friends and greeting strangers in the table below.

和不认识的人打招呼	和老朋友打招呼
(1) 你好！你叫什么？	(1) 你好！好久不见了！
(2) 你的爱好是什么？	(2) 你最近忙吗？
(3)	(3)

Communication task

1. Describe the appearance of these poople.

   Example:
   杰克高高的，瘦瘦的，喜欢运动，长得很帅(shuài，handsome)。

杰克

2. Divide into groups, with three students in each group. Each person will make a card like the examples shown. On the left side of the card, write information about yourself. On the right side of the card, write information about the person to your right. Mix your three cards with other groups. Ask your classmates questions in order to find out which friend is being described by the information on the right side.

你长得高吗？你戴不戴眼镜？你叫Linda吗？……

Example:

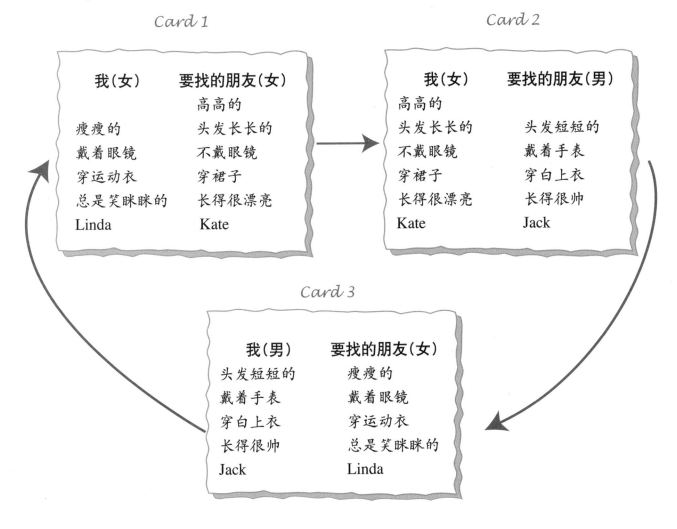

Card 1

我（女）	要找的朋友（女）
	高高的
瘦瘦的	头发长长的
戴着眼镜	不戴眼镜
穿运动衣	穿裙子
总是笑眯眯的	长得很漂亮
Linda	Kate

Card 2

我（女）	要找的朋友（男）
高高的	
头发长长的	头发短短的
不戴眼镜	戴着手表
穿裙子	穿白上衣
长得很漂亮	长得很帅
Kate	Jack

Card 3

我（男）	要找的朋友（女）
头发短短的	瘦瘦的
戴着手表	戴着眼镜
穿白上衣	穿运动衣
长得很帅	总是笑眯眯的
Jack	Linda

Reading and comprehension

Choose the one that continues or completes the sentence in a logical and culturally appropriate manner by mark √.

1. 李先生是美华的爸爸，他戴着眼镜，经常笑眯眯的，*我们很喜欢他。*

① 昨天他的儿子回来了。（   ）

② 他一直在说话。（   ）

③ 我们很喜欢他。(✓)

④ 我们没看见他。( )

2. 马明暑假很忙，过得不错，他帮着邻居搬家，他的邻居 <u>刚从香港来。</u>

① 刚从香港来。(✓)

② 好久不见了。( )

③ 过得挺好。( )

④ 就是喜欢踢足球。( )

Listen and practice

1. Listening Comprehension

(1) Decide whether the following statements are true or false after listening to the recording.

① 王太太是我爸爸的朋友。(✗) ✓

② 王太太和她的先生有一个女儿。(✓) ✓

③ 王太太矮矮的，胖胖的。(✗) ✓

④ 王太太的先生经常笑眯眯的。(✗) ✓

⑤ 小美的眼睛很大。(✓) ✓

⑥ 王太太的女儿今年 4 岁。(✓) ✓

(2) Answer the following questions after listening to the recording.

Key words:

停 tíng (to park) 门口 ménkǒu (doorway)

男孩儿 nánháir (boy) 汉堡包 hànbǎobāo (hamburger)

还 huán (to return)

Questions:

① 谁把车停在商店门口？ 李先生

② 他为什么把车停在商店门口？ 他 哦了

③ 他给了男孩儿什么？为什么？ ràng 他买两个 汉堡包.

④ 他对男孩儿说什么？ 买两个汉堡包

⑤ 半个小时以后男孩儿做了什么？ 买了两子汉堡包.

⑥ 李先生吃到汉堡包了吗？ 没有.

10

2. Read the following modern poem.

远　远　的　街　灯　明　了，
yuǎn yuǎn de jiē dēng míng le

好　像　闪　着　无　数　的　明　星。
hǎo xiàng shǎn zhe wú shù de míng xīng

天　上　的　明　星　现　了，
tiān shàng de míng xīng xiàn le

好　像　点　着　无　数　的　街　灯。
hǎo xiàng diǎn zhe wú shù de jiē dēng

我　想　那　缥　缈　的　空　中，
wǒ xiǎng nà piāo miǎo de kōng zhōng

定　然　有　美　丽　的　街　市。
dìng rán yǒu měi lì de jiē shì

街　市　上　陈　列　的　一　些　物　品，
jiē shì shang chén liè de yì xiē wù pǐn

定　然　是　世　上　没　有　的　珍　奇。
dìng rán shì shì shàng méi yǒu de zhēn qí

（节选自郭沫若《天上的街市》）

> The streetlights brightened afar,
> Like the countless twinkling stars.
> The stars in the sky appeared,
> Like numerous burning streetlights.
>
> I fancy there must be a beautiful city,
> Up in the misty space.
> The objects displayed there must be treasures,
> That do not exist in our earthy place.

Chinese characters

Write new characters on the stairs with the number of strokes decreasing one by one.

Oriental Pearl — Hong Kong

Located in the south of China, Hong Kong consists of Hong Kong Island, Kowloon Peninsula, New Territories and many other islands. Covering an area of 1104 square kilometers and with a population of over 7 million, Hong Kong is a world-renowned international metropolis. Hong Kong used to be a British colony from 1842 to 1997 when China resumed the exercise of sovereignty and set up the "Hong Kong Special Administrative Region". Hong Kong is a place where Chinese and western cultures meet, and it is also an important transportation hub and one of the most competitive cities which leads the world in the Index of Economic Freedom. As the world's third largest financial center next only to London and New York, Hong Kong also enjoys the reputation of being an "Oriental Pearl" and a "Shopping Heaven".

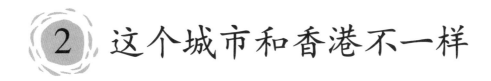

2 这个城市和香港不一样

Getting started

Can you tell the difference between the two cities?

Text 1

Jack drops in at Meiyun's place.

杰克：美云，你好！

美云：你好！请进！

杰克：今天学校有晚会，请你去参加。

美云：谢谢你来通知我。

杰克：不客气，你刚搬来，我也想过来看看。

美云：好，我带你参观一下我的新家。

杰克：谢谢。

美云：我家的卧室(wòshì)在楼上(lóu shang)，客厅(kètīng)和厨房(chúfáng)在楼下(lóu xià)。我最喜欢的地方是我家的厨房。每天早晨我们一起床就(yī...jiù)去厨房，在那儿一边吃早饭，一边(yìbiān...yìbiān)看新闻(xīnwén)。吃完早饭，大家就各自(gèzì)去上班(shàngbān)、上学。晚上一家人又(yòu)会在厨房见面。

杰克：真好，你在香港的家不是这样吗？

美云：不太一样。快请坐，请喝茶。

杰克：谢谢。

Text 2

Meiyun is writing to one of her friends in Hong Kong.

亲爱的小梅(Xiǎoméi)：你好！

我们家搬到这里已经两个月了。这里的夏天跟香港一样热，不过热的时间没有香港长。这个城市(chéngshì)跟香港很不一样，比香港小，人口(rénkǒu)没有香港的多。在香港一出门(chūmén)就能看见商店(shāngdiàn)；在这里，大家都去超市(chāoshì)买东西。在香港，马路(mǎlù)两边(biān)有很多卖(mài)早餐(zǎocān)的小吃店(xiǎochīdiàn)；早晨上学的时候，我们常常在那里吃早餐。可是这里的人都在家里吃早餐。现在我已经习惯(xíguàn)在家里吃早餐了。

现在我家有了自己的院子(yuànzi)，每个星期天我和弟弟都把院子打扫得干干净净。我们在新家生活得很愉快。

请代(dài)我向朋友们问好(wènhǎo)！

祝你万事如意(wànshì rúyì)！

你的好朋友：李美云

9月8日

New words

1.	卧室	wòshì	*n.*	bedroom
2.	楼上	lóu shang		upstairs
3.	客厅	kètīng	*n.*	living room
4.	厨房	chúfáng	*n.*	kitchen
5.	楼下	lóu xià		downstairs
6.	一……就……	yī...jiù...		no sooner than...; as soon as...; the minute...
7.	一边……一边……	yìbiān...yìbiān...		as... (used to join two parallel actions)
8.	新闻	xīnwén	*n.*	news
9.	各自	gèzì	*pron.*	separately；on one's own
10.	上班	shàngbān	*v.*	to go to work
11.	又	yòu	*adv.*	again
12.	城市	chéngshì	*n.*	city
13.	人口	rénkǒu	*n.*	population
14.	出门	chūmén	*v.*	to go out
15.	商店	shāngdiàn	*n.*	shop; store
16.	超市	chāoshì	*n.*	supermarket
17.	马路	mǎlù	*n.*	road; street
18.	边	biān	*n.*	side
19.	卖	mài	*v.*	to sell
20.	早餐	zǎocān	*n.*	breakfast
21.	小吃店	xiǎochīdiàn	*n.*	snack bar
22.	习惯	xíguàn	*n./v.*	habit / to be used to
23.	院子	yuànzi	*n.*	courtyard
24.	代	dài	*v.*	to be on behalf of
25.	问好	wènhǎo	*v.*	to send one's regards to
26.	万事如意	wànshì rúyì		everything goes as you wish

Proper noun

小梅	Xiǎoméi	Xiaomei

16

Notes

1. "每天早晨我们一起床就去厨房。"

The "一……就……" structure is usually used to describe that the first action just finishes and is immediately followed by the second action.

弟弟一回家就跑去喂狗。

我一上完课就去看电影了。

2. "在那儿一边吃早饭，一边看新闻。"

The structure "一边……一边……" usually describes that the two actions take place at the same time.

他一边吃饭，一边看电视。

我们一边走，一边看，心情特别好。

3. "人口没有香港的多。"

This sentence means the population in Hong Kong is more than that in this city. It is also a comparison sentence. For example, 我没有他高 means 他比我高.

这个人没有那个人热情。

昨天没有今天热。

Exercise

On your own

1. Match the left and right columns to form 5 sentences based on the text.

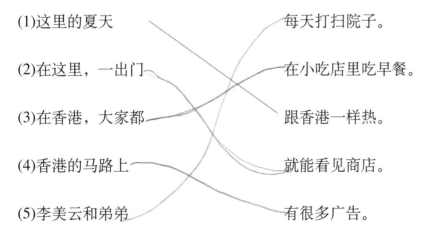

(1)这里的夏天　　　　　　　每天打扫院子。

(2)在这里，一出门　　　　　在小吃店里吃早餐。

(3)在香港，大家都　　　　　跟香港一样热。

(4)香港的马路上　　　　　　就能看见商店。

(5)李美云和弟弟　　　　　　有很多广告。

2. Word Classification

Classify the following words into four categories.

(1) 厨房 _chufang_   (2) 狗 _gou_   (3) 脸 _lian_   (4) 报纸 _baozhi_   (5) 眼睛 _yanjing_   (6) 乌龟 _wugui_

(7) 客厅 _keting_   (8) 电视 _dianshi_   (9) 眼镜 _yanjing_   (10) 猫 _mao_   (11) 盒子 _hezi_   (12) 卧室 _woshi_

Animals   _狗 猫 乌龟_   Rooms   _卧室 厨房 客厅_

Human organs   _脸 眼睛_   Objects   _报纸 眼镜 盒子 电视_

Conversation practice

1. Look at the pictures, use "一……就……" in your conversation exercises.

    A：你看到小猫会怎么样?

    B：我一看到小猫就很喜欢。

2. What are the people in the pictures doing?

Try to describe each picture with the phrase "一边……一边……", then make a conversation with your partner.

3. Make a comparison.

Compare the pictures of the two cities to find the similarities and differences between them, then make a conversation with your partner with sentence pattern "有/没有"and "A比B+形容词+ '多了' ".

Class activity & communication task

My Home

Make groups of three. One student describes the layout of his/her home and the other two draw a picture of the house according to the description. Select three pictures that best suit the description, then compare the difference of the drawings.

Reading and comprehension

1. Multiple choice

"我们家和这里不一样，天气没有这么热，街上没有这么多人，车子也没这么多，不过草地比这里多。" 不过 in this sentence means (   ).

A. 而且   B. 不但   C. 但是   D. 可是

2. True or False

(1) 我一回去就给他打电话，让他秋天来。

　　　⟹ 因为我要回去，所以我得给他打电话。（　）

(2) 一看见老师，他就说不出话来。

　　　⟹ 只要看见老师，他就很紧张(jǐnzhāng, nervous, tense)。（　）

Listen and practice

1. Listening comprehension

(1) Decide whether the following statements are true or false after listening to the recording.
① 我家的卧室在楼下。（　）

② 每天晚上我们都在客厅见面。（　）

③ 爸爸喜欢一边喝茶一边大声地说话。（　）

④ 爸爸想知道我和妹妹每天在学校干什么。（　）

⑤ 爸爸妈妈在客厅里，我和妹妹在厨房。（　）

⑥ 我和妹妹常常一起在客厅看电视。（　）

(2) Answer the following questions after listening to the recording.

Key words:

下雪	xiàxuě	snow
超市	chāoshì	supermarket
早点	zǎodiǎn	breakfast
摊位	tānwèi	booth
换着样儿	huànzhe yàngr	in different ways
油条	yóutiáo	fried dough sticks
煎饼	jiānbǐng	pancake

Questions:

① 说话人所住城市的天气与北京的天气有什么不同？北京 gèn léng.

② 北京只有超市吗？不是。

③ 北京人早点吃什么？

④ 说话人习惯这个城市的生活了吗？不习惯。

2. Read the following tongue twister.

路 东 住 着 刘 小 柳，
lù dōng zhù zhe liú xiǎo liǔ

路 南 住 着 牛 小 妞。
lù nán zhù zhe niú xiǎo niū

刘 小 柳 和 牛 小 妞，
liú xiǎo liǔ hé niú xiǎo niū

她 们 俩 是 好 朋 友。
tā men liǎ shì hǎo péng you

Liu Xiaoliu lives on the east side of the road.

Niu Xiaoniu lives on the south side of the road.

Liu Xiaoliu and Niu Xiaoniu are good pals.

Chinese characters

Let's play a game of combining and separating characters.

日月（ 明 ），（ 鱼 ）（ 羊 ）鲜。

（ 小 ）（ 土 ）尘，（ 小 ）（ 大 ）尖。

（ 一 ）（ 火 ）灭，田力（ 男 ）。

人木（ 休 ），手目（ 看 ）。

二木（ 林 ），三木（ 森 ）。

二人（ 从 ），（ 人 ）（ 从 ）众。

3 弟弟的宠物(chǒngwù)

Getting started

What kinds of animals do you think can be your pets?

If you keep such animals as pets, where would you keep them?

蜘蛛 (zhīzhū)

刺猬 (cìwei)

狐狸 (húli)

画眉鸟 (huàméi niǎo)

乌鸦 (wūyā)

狗 (gǒu)

老虎 (lǎohǔ)

麻雀 (máquè)

鹰 (yīng)

猫 (māo)

狮子 (shīzi)

狼 (láng)

鱼 (yú)

蛇 (shé)

寻找 (xúnzhǎo) 猫的主人 (zhǔrén)

一只黄色的小猫 (xiǎomāo)，眼睛是蓝色的，四只爪子 (zhuǎzi) 是白色的。如果您丢 (diū) 了一只这样的猫，请打下面的电话：653-8854。

Text 1

Meiyun is making a suggestion to Meihua.

美云：美华，我有个建议。

美华：什么建议？

美云：把狗关(guān)在你的房间(fángjiān)里①，好吗？

美华：为什么？

美云：它会咬(yǎo)人的。每次看见我的朋友，它都大喊大叫(dà hǎn dà jiào)。

美华：好吧。不过，我也有个建议。

美云：什么建议？

美华：把我的乌龟(wūguī)和鹦鹉(yīngwǔ)放在你的房间里，怎么样？

美云：为什么？

美华：如果狗看见乌龟和鹦鹉，它也会大喊大叫的。

① 把狗关在你的房间里：Keep the dog in your room

Text 2

Ma Ming drops in. Meiyun is telling him about the pets in her brother's room.

我弟弟非常喜欢养(yǎng)宠物。他养着许多动物。如果你去他的房间，一定(yídìng)要小心(xiǎoxīn)。他的狗总是在门口(ménkǒu)蹲(dūn)着。窗户的旁边有一只鹦鹉，一看见你，它就会问(wèn)："你是谁？"桌子下面放着一个盒子(hézi)，里面(lǐmiàn)有两只乌龟。有时候(yǒu shíhou)，它们会出(chū)来，如果你不小心踩(cǎi)到(dào)它们，你就会摔跤(shuāijiāo)。

New words

1. 宠物	chǒngwù	*n.*	pet
2. 关	guān	*v.*	to shut
3. 房间	fángjiān	*n.*	room
4. 咬	yǎo	*v.*	to bite
5. 大喊大叫	dà hǎn dà jiào		to shout at the top of one's voice
6. 乌龟	wūguī	*n.*	tortoise
7. 鹦鹉	yīngwǔ	*n.*	parrot
8. 养	yǎng	*v.*	to raise; to keep (as a pet)
9. 一定	yídìng	*adv.*	certainly; surely; definitely
10. 小心	xiǎoxīn	*v.*	to mind; to watch out; to be careful
11. 门口	ménkǒu	*n.*	doorway
12. 蹲	dūn	*v.*	to squat
13. 问	wèn	*v.*	to ask
14. 盒子	hézi	*n.*	box
15. 里面	lǐmiàn	*n.*	inside
16. 有时候	yǒu shíhou		sometimes
17. 出	chū	*v.*	to exit; to go/come out
18. 踩	cǎi	*v.*	to step on; to trample
19. 到	dào	*v.*	*used as a verb complement to show the result of an action*
20. 摔跤	shuāijiāo	*v.*	to tumble; to trip and fall

Notes

1. "把狗关在你的房间里，好吗？"

   This is a 把 sentence, but what's different from the 把 sentence with appeared in Book Two is that the verb is followed by a prepositional structure "在……房间里" indicating location.

   妈妈把画儿挂在墙上。

   司机把车停在路边。

2. "它会咬人的。"

   We studied the auxiliary verb 会 indicating having the ability to do something in Lesson 27 of Book One. While in this sentence, 会 means something is possible.

   你会慢慢喜欢上它的。

   天气会变冷的。

3. "他养着许多动物。"

   The particle 着，put after the verb, indicates the action in progress or a continuation of a state.

   他在路上慢慢地走着。（动作正在进行）

   教室的门紧紧地关着。（状态的持续）

Exercise

On your own

Describe the pictures with " Verb + 着" structure, using the verbs given.

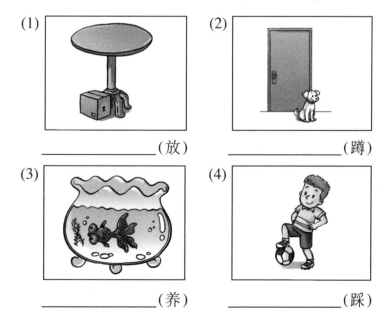

(1) ＿＿＿＿＿＿＿（放）　　(2) ＿＿＿＿＿＿＿（蹲）

(3) ＿＿＿＿＿＿＿（养）　　(4) ＿＿＿＿＿＿＿（踩）

Conversation practice

1. Make new conversations according to the given example. Practice with a partner.

A：我有个建议，我们去_____?

B：_____。

A：那我们去看电影吧。

B：好啊。

---
① 吃肯德基(to have KFC)　不喜欢吃肯德基　吃麦当劳

② 吃中餐　不喜欢吃中餐　吃西餐

③ 买衣服　不喜欢买东西　打网球
---

2. In pairs role play discussing suggestions. One student make a suggestion to do something, the other disagrees. Then both students can negotiate and come to a solution.

Class activity & communication task

1. Matching animal cards

The whole class recalls the names of the animals they have learned in Chinese and then write down these names and their *pinyin* on the blackboard. Four to six people in a group make two sets of cards, one in Chinese characters and the other in *pinyin*. Mix the cards with their faces down. Pick up two cards each time and turn them over to see if the characters match the *pinyin*. If they don't, turn them back again, and the other student begins his / her turn. If the characters match the *pinyin*, the person who turns them over wins the two cards. The one who has the most cards wins the game.

2. Finishing actions

Work in groups of three to four people. Gather together cups, books, mobile phones and pens of the students. One student gives instructions using "把" sentence, and other students act out quickly and finish the action based on the instructions. Try to act both quickly and correctly.

Example:

请把杯子放到/在桌子上。

请把书放到/在书包里。

Read and talk

黔驴技穷 (qiánlǘ-jìqióng，The Guizhou Donkey's Tricks)

以前有一个地方叫"黔"(qián, Guizhou)，那里没有驴(lǘ, donkey)。有人把一头驴运到那里，放在山下。老虎(tiger)看见驴又高又大，很害怕(hàipà, to be scared)。有一天，老虎听到驴的叫声，更害怕了。可是过了几天，老虎习惯了。它走到驴的身边碰(pèng, to touch)碰驴。驴生气了，用蹄子(tízi, hoof)踢老虎。老虎很高兴，它明白了，驴只会用蹄子踢，于是它就把驴吃了。

Questions:

① 老虎为什么没有一见到驴就把它吃了？

② 老虎后来为什么很高兴？

Listen and practice

1. Listening comprehension

   (1) Decide whether the following statements are true or false after listening to the recording.

   ① 我的朋友养的动物不多。(✗)

   ② 桌子上是猫睡觉的地方。(✗)

   ③ 狗在椅子上休息。(✓)

   ④ 鹦鹉站在窗户的旁边。(✓)

   ⑤ 乌龟在椅子下面。(✗)

   ⑥ 我的朋友有八只猫。(✓)

   (2) Answer the following questions after listening to the recording.

   Key words:

   依赖 yīlài (to rely on)　　　　照顾 zhàogù (to look after)

   适合 shìhé (suitable)　　　　遛 liù (to go for a walk)

   Questions:

   ① 男的提出了什么问题？

   ② 为什么男的不适合养狗？

   ③ 男的适合养什么？

   ④ "就这样决定了"是什么意思？

2. Read the following children's song.

树 姥 姥，最 爱 鸟，一 群 一 群 飞 来 了。
shù lǎo lao zuì ài niǎo yì qún yì qún fēi lái liǎo

什 么 鸟，布 谷 鸟，千 家 万 户 把 春 报。
shén me niǎo bù gǔ niǎo qiān jiā wàn hù bǎ chūn bào

什 么 鸟，百 灵 鸟，唱 红 杏 花 唱 红 桃。
shén me niǎo bǎi líng niǎo chàng hóng xìng huā chàng hóng táo

什 么 鸟，猫 头 鹰，捉 只 田 鼠 吃 个 饱。
shén me niǎo māo tóu yīng zhuō zhī tián shǔ chī gè bǎo

树 姥 姥，最 爱 鸟，一 群 一 群 怀 里 抱。
shù lǎo lao zuì ài niǎo yì qún yì qún huái li bào

The old granny tree loves birds most. She's happy to see them come over in groups. What type of bird? Cuckoos, telling everyone spring comes. What type of bird? Larks, bringing about the blossoms of apricots and peaches. What type of bird? Owls, stuffing their stomachs with rats. The old granny tree loves birds most, holding them in an embrace.

Writing

Two Families

Make groups of 4-6 students. Conduct a survey about 2 of the students' families including the appearance and hobbies of each of the family members, their habits and daily routines and the layout of their homes and the pets they keep. Then compare the similarities and differences between the two families.

"两个家庭"调查表

A Survey of Two Families

	Family 1	Family 2
Address		
Family Members		
Family Member's Appearance		
Family Member's Hobbies		
House Layout		
Pets		
Habits and Daily Schedules		
Survey Conductor		
Survey Time		

Chinese characters

Look at the picture and guess the word.

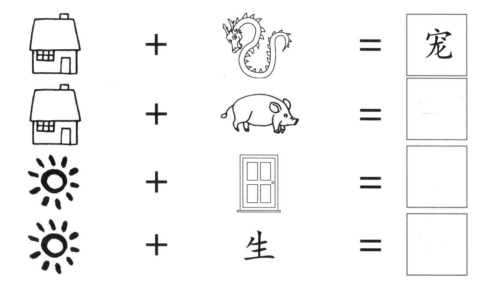

Giant Panda

As an animal species unique to China and a first class protected animal at the state level, giant panda is reputed as "China's national treasure". The pandas are also endangered animals protected in the world. At present, there are up to 1, 600 wild pandas and over 300 captive ones. Their habitats are mostly located in the mountains in Sichuan, Shaanxi and Gansu in China.

Having survived on earth for at least 8 million years, pandas are regarded as "living fossils". They used to eat meat at the very beginning, but have evolved to mainly rely on bamboo for food. Wild pandas have a life span of 18 to 20 years, while captive pandas can live beyond the age of 30. Pandas are lovely creatures well-known for their black and white colors, round face, big dark circles around their eyes, and a fat body shape.

UNIT SUMMARY

FUNCTIONAL USAGE

1. Old friends greeting each other

好 久 不 见!
hǎo jiǔ bú jiàn

2. Describing appearances

他 高 高 的，瘦 瘦 的，戴 着 一 副 眼 镜。
tā gāo gāo de shòu shòu de dài zhe yí fù yǎn jìng

3. Describing the layout of the home

我 家 的 卧 室 在 楼 上，客 厅 和 厨 房 在 楼 下。
wǒ jiā de wò shì zài lóu shang kè tīng hé chú fáng zài lóu xià

4. Offering suggestions

我 有 个 建 议。
wǒ yǒu gè jiàn yì

GRAMMAR FOCUS

Sentence pattern	*Example*
1. 副词"就"	她 就 是 我 邻 居 的 女 儿。 tā jiù shì wǒ lín jū de nǔ ér
2. 形容词重叠	他 高 高 的，瘦 瘦 的。 tā gāo gāo de shòushòu de
3. 动词＋"得"＋……	她 长 得 很 漂 亮。 tā zhǎng de hěn piàoliang
4. "一……就……"	请 你 一 到 家 就 给 我 打 电 话。 qǐng nǐ yí dào jiā jiù gěi wǒ dǎ diàn huà
5. "一边……一边……"	他 一 边 喝 咖 啡，一 边 看 报 纸。 tā yì biān hē kā fēi yì biān kàn bào zhǐ
6. A没有B＋形容词	这 个 城 市 的 人 口 没 有 香 港 多。 zhè ge chéng shì de rén kǒu méi yǒu xiāng gǎng duō
7. "把"＋宾语＋动词 ＋处所补语	把 狗 关 在 你 的 房 间 里。 bǎ gǒu guān zài nǐ de fáng jiān li
8. 助动词"会"	它 会 咬 人 的。 tā huì yǎo rén de
9. 动词＋"着"	他 养 着 很 多 宠 物。 tā yǎng zhe hěn duō chǒng wù

CHINESE CHARACTERS REVIEW

汉字 Chinese character		拼音 *Pinyin*	词语组合 Language composition
帮	邦 巾	bāng	帮助　帮忙
搬	扌 般	bān	搬家　搬东西
邻	令 阝	lín	邻居　相邻
笑	竹 夭	xiào	笑眯眯　笑容
常	尚 巾	cháng	经常　非常
话	讠 舌	huà	说话　会话
室	宀 至	shì	教室　办公室
楼	木 娄	lóu	楼房　楼梯
厅	厂 丁	tīng	客厅　餐厅
惯	忄 贯	guàn	习惯　惯性
跟	足 艮	gēn	跟从　跟随
餐	𣥂 食	cān	餐厅　中餐
议	讠 义	yì	会议　议论

Unit Two

Leisure Time

4 我也想到中国去

Getting started

Can you complete the following form in Chinese?

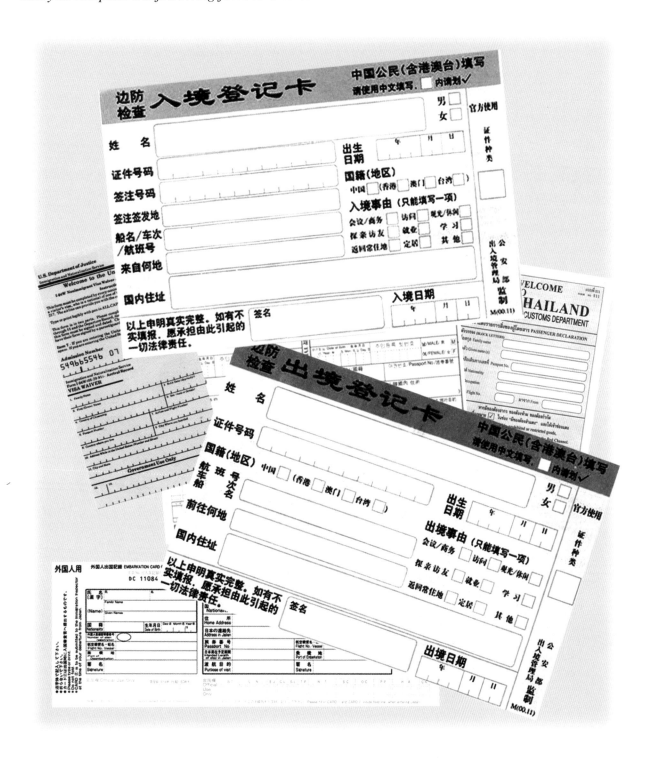

37

Text 1

David is calling Jack.

大卫：你好，请问，杰克在不在?

杰克：我就是杰克。请问你是谁?

大卫：我是大卫。你还记得 (jìde) 我吗?

杰克：哦，当然。好久没 (méi) 听到你的消息 (xiāoxi) 了。你到哪儿去 (dào...qù) 了?

大卫：我到中国去了，上个星期①才回来。

杰克：是吗，你去了哪些 (nǎxiē) 地方?

大卫：我去了北京、西安 (Xī'ān) 、上海 (Shànghǎi) 、苏州 (Sūzhōu) 、杭州 (Hángzhōu)……

杰克：啊，你去了那么多地方! 你拍照片了吗?

大卫：当然了，我拍了很多照片。我还要送给你一件礼物呢。

杰克：太好了，谢谢你。

① 上个星期：last week

Text 2

Jack is telling Ma Ming about David's travelling in China.

　　前天 (qiántiān) 大卫来我家，他进(jìn)来的时候，我差点儿 (chàdiǎnr) 没认出他来。我们已经一年没有见面了。他现在个子 (gèzi) 很高，也瘦了许多 (xǔduō)，更帅 (shuài) 了。

　　去年他到中国去了，他在北京学习了一年呢。现在他说汉语说得非常好①。这一年，大卫还参观(cānguān) 了许多名胜古迹 (míngshèng gǔjì)。他去西安参观了秦始皇兵马俑 (Qínshǐhuáng Bīngmǎyǒng)。他说黄果树瀑布 (Huángguǒshù Pùbù)也很漂亮，不过没有尼亚加拉瀑布 (Níyàjiālā Pùbù) 那么大。他还从中国给我带(dài)来一个礼物呢。我很羡慕(xiànmù)他，我也想到中国去。

---

① 他说汉语说得非常好：He speaks Chinese very well

39

New words

1. 记得	jìde	*v.*	to remember
2. 没	méi	*adv.*	have not; do not
3. 消息	xiāoxi	*n.*	news
4. 到……去	dào...qù		to go to ...
5. 哪些	nǎxiē	*pron.*	which (ones); who; what
6. 前天	qiántiān	*n.*	the day before yesterday
7. 进	jìn	*v.*	to enter
8. 差点儿	chàdiǎnr	*adv.*	almost
9. 个子	gèzi	*n.*	stature
10. 许多	xǔduō	*adj.*	a lot; a great deal
11. 帅	shuài	*adj.*	handsome
12. 参观	cānguān	*v.*	to visit
13. 名胜古迹	míngshèng gǔjì		scenic spots and historic sites
14. 瀑布	pùbù	*n.*	waterfall
15. 带	dài	*v.*	to bring
16. 羡慕	xiànmù	*v.*	to envy; to admire

Proper nouns

1. 西安	Xī'ān	Xi'an
2. 上海	Shànghǎi	Shanghai
3. 苏州	Sūzhōu	Suzhou
4. 杭州	Hángzhōu	Hangzhou
5. 秦始皇兵马俑	Qínshǐhuáng Bīngmǎyǒng	terracotta warriors and horses in the tomb of Emperor Qinshihuang
6. 黄果树瀑布	Huángguǒshù Pùbù	the Huangguoshu Waterfall
7. 尼亚加拉瀑布	Níyàjiālā Pùbù	Niagara Falls

Notes

1. "我也想到中国去。"

去 in this sentence, put after the main verb 到, indicates the direction of an action and is called a directional complement. 中国 is the object of 到. 来 may also serve as a directional complement. 来 is used when the action moves towards the direction of the speaker, and 去 is used for the opposite situation.

他向教室走来。(说话人在教室)

他向教室走去。(说话人不在教室)

他回北京来了。(说话人在北京)

他回北京去了。(说话人没在北京)

2. "我差点儿没认出他来。"

差点儿 is an adverb indicating something that is nearly realized or something that is fully realized after some difficulty. The exact meaning of 差点儿 is determined by the context.

他差点儿迟到。(没迟到)

他差点儿没买到电影票。(买到了)

3. "现在他说汉语说得非常好。"

This is a sentence with the same verb repeated. The sentence pattern is that a verb is followed by an object, then the same verb is repeated which is followed by a complementary part.

他吃饺子吃得可香了。

他跳舞跳得好极了。

Exercise

On your own

1. Match the left and right columns to form 4 sentences.

(1) 大卫到中国   来参观。

(2) 大卫和杰克已经一年   来了一个礼物。

(3) 很多中国学生到我们学校   去了。

(4) 大卫从中国给杰克带   没有见面了。

2. Choose one word from "去" "来" to form a correct sentence according to the given pictures.

电影快开始了，同学们进 ＿＿＿＿＿ 了。

电影结束了，大家从电影院里出 ＿＿＿＿＿ 了。✓

我能进 ＿＿＿＿＿ 吗？ ✓

我能出 ＿＿＿＿＿ 玩吗？

Conversation practice

1. Make a conversation with your partner. Use sentences with the same verb repeated based on the given sentences.

例如： 他汉语很好。 ⟹ A：他汉语怎么样？ B：他说汉语说得非常好。

他写字太慢了。 ⟹ A：＿＿＿＿＿＿＿＿＿？ B：＿＿＿＿＿＿＿＿＿。

他睡觉太晚了。 ⟹ A：＿＿＿＿＿＿＿＿＿？ B：＿＿＿＿＿＿＿＿＿。

他看书太累了。 ⟹ A：＿＿＿＿＿＿＿＿＿？ B：＿＿＿＿＿＿＿＿＿。

Class activity & communication task

1. Work in groups. Make a PPT in advance based on the following clues. Discuss the questions.

> Where have you visited as a tourist? Please prepare a PPT document at home and show your classmates the pictures you took. You should share the following information with your classmates:
>
> (1) Where did you go?
>
> (2) When did you go?
>
> (3) How did you go?
>
> (4) Who did you go with?
>
> (5) What were the most interesting things?

2. Share your travel experience with the class.

Reading comprehension

1. 老师让我给孩子买一本书，我差点儿忘了。我下午到书店去，买这本书的人太多了，我差点儿没买到。最后我还是给了孩子一个惊喜(surprise)。

   (1) "我差点儿忘了"意思是(　　)。　A. 忘了　　　　　　B. 没有忘

   (2) "我差点儿没买到"意思是(　　)。　A. 买到书了　　　　B. 没买到书

2. 名落孙山(míng luò Sūn Shān，Fall behind Sun Shan, Fail in a competitive examination)

   古时候有个人叫孙山，他很喜欢开玩笑。有一天，他和邻居的儿子一起去参加科举考试(kējǔ kǎoshì, imperial examinations)，结果他考中(kǎozhòng, to pass an exam)了，但在考中的人中，他是最后一名(zuìhòu yì míng, the last in the rank)。邻居的儿子没有考中，不好意思回家。孙山回到家，邻居来问自己的儿子考得怎么样。孙山说，在考中的人中，孙山是最后一名，您儿子的名字还在孙山的后面。

   True or False:

   (1)孙山通过了考试。(　　)

   (2)邻居的儿子是考中的人当中最后一名。(　　)

Listen and practice

1. Listening comprehension

   (1) Decide whether the following statements are true or false after listening to the recording.

   Key words:

   王小雨 Wang Xiaoyu   云南 Yunnan

   西双版纳 Xishuangbanna   泼水节 the Water-Splashing Festival

   大理 Dali

   True or false:

   ① 王小雨是杰克以前的同学。(   )

   ② 杰克不认识王小雨。(   )

   ③ 王小雨以前又高又瘦。(   )

   ④ 王小雨去大理参加了泼水节。(   )

   ⑤ 西双版纳 (Xīshuāngbǎnnà) 比大理 (Dàlǐ) 大。(   )

   ⑥ 王小雨在中国住了一年。(   )

   (2) Answer the following questions after listening to the recording.

   Key words:

   地理课 dìlǐkè (geography)   问题 wèntí (question)

   世界 shìjiè (world)   山 shān (mountain)

   二郎山 Èrláng Shān (Erlang Mountain)   奇怪 qíguài (strange)

   唱一支歌 chàng yì zhī gē (to sing a song)   歌词 gēcí (lyrics)

   一丈等于3 米 yí zhàng děngyú sān mǐ (one zhang equals to 3 meters)

   万丈就等于 30,000 米 wàn zhàng jiù děngyú sān wàn mǐ

   (then 10,000 zhang is 30,000 meters)

   第一高峰珠穆朗玛峰 dì-yī gāofēng Zhūmùlángmǎ Fēng

   (the world's highest mountain, Mt. Everest)

   Questions:

   ① 老师问了什么问题?

   ② 美华为什么认为二郎山是最高的山?

44

③ 你听说过二郎山吗？

④ 老师是不是讲错了？为什么？

⑤ 你认为美华说得对不对？为什么？

2. Read the following ancient poem.

朝　辞　白　帝　彩　云　间，
zhāo cí bái dì cǎi yún jiān

千　里　江　陵　一　日　还。
qiān lǐ jiāng líng yí rì huán

两　岸　猿　声　啼　不　住，
liǎng àn yuán shēng tí bú zhù

轻　舟　已　过　万　重　山。
qīng zhōu yǐ guò wàn chóng shān

(唐·李白《早发白帝城》)

Leaving at dawn the White Emperor crowned with cloud,
I've sailed a thousand *li* through Canyons in a day.
With the monkeys' adieus the riverbanks are loud,
My skiff has left ten thousand mountains far away.

Chinese characters

Choose the proper characters and fill in the blanks.

(1) 　　邻　暑　搬　女

（　）假　（　）孩　（　）居　（　）家

(2) 　　瀑　参　启　照

（　）事　（　）片　（　）布　（　）观

(3) 　　盒　乌　蹲　建

（　）着　（　）子　（　）议　（　）龟

The Terracotta Warriors of the First Emperor
Qin Shihuang's Mausoleum

Located in the Lintong area 35 km east of Xi'an City Shaanxi Province, the Terracotta Warriors are found in the pits in the Mausoleum of the First Chinese Emperor Ying Zheng. The terracotta army was discovered in 1974 by local farmers when they were digging a well.

Built between 246 BC to 208 BC, the Mausoleum is huge in size and perfectly designed, including underground palaces, sealing earth, cities, gates, and pits. Nearly 8,000 clay warriors and horses the size of real man and horse are found. There are also orderly arranged chariot soldiers, cavalrymen, infantrymen and other arms of the army. Presenting different images, the terracotta army is reputed both as the "the Eighth Wonder of the World" and "one of the greatest archaeological findings in the 20th Century".

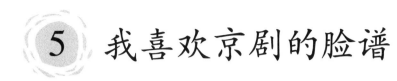

5 我喜欢京剧的脸谱

Getting Started

Let's learn a little about the following types of facial makeup in the Peking opera and the stories in which they appear.

中国京剧院演出

(Performance by China Opera House)

《空 城 计》

(The Stratagem of the Empty City)

诸葛亮 Zhuge Liang —— 由……扮演
(played by ...)

司马懿 Sima Yi —— 由……扮演
(played by ...)

时间 (Time):
星期一、三、五晚上7:30
(7:30 pm, Monday, Wednesday, Friday)

票价 (Ticket Price):
20 — 80 元 (￥ 20 — 80)

Text 1

Jack and Meiyun are in front of a theatre; Ma Ming is coming out of the ticket office…

美云： 马明，你买到票了吗？

马明： 只买到了两张票。看京剧 (jīngjù) 的人太多了。

美云： 那怎么办 (zěnme bàn) ？

杰克： 马明，你和美云先进去，我在这儿等退票 (tuìpiào)。

美云： 没有退票怎么办？

杰克： 不会的①。虽然售票处 (shòupiàochù) 没有票了，但是 (suīrán... dànshì...) 一定会有人来退票。

马明： 好吧②，我们进去等你，你一买到票就进来。

杰克： 放心 (fàngxīn) 进去吧，一会儿 (yíhuìr) 见。

---

① 不会的：be unlikely; will not (act, happen, etc.)

② 好吧：OK; all right

49

Text 2

Ma Ming's diary — talking about the Peking opera.

前天，我和杰克、美云一起看了一场(chǎng)京剧。看京剧的年轻人(niánqīngrén)不多，中学生更少。我想他们跟我一样，看不懂(dǒng)。不过，听说(tīngshuō)现在喜欢京剧的年轻人逐渐(zhújiàn)多起来了。虽然我看不懂京剧，但是我喜欢看各种各样(gèzhǒng gèyàng)的脸谱(liǎnpǔ)和武打(wǔdǎ)，也喜欢听京剧的音乐。

New words

1. 京剧	jīngjù	*n.*	Peking opera
2. 怎么办	zěnme bàn		how (to do)
3. 退票	tuìpiào	*v.*	to return ticket
4. 售票处	shòupiàochù	*n.*	ticket office
5. 虽然……但是……	suīrán...dànshì...		although; but
6. 放心	fàngxīn	*v.*	to set one's mind at rest; to rest assured
7. 一会儿	yíhuìr		a little while (later); in a minute
8. 场	chǎng	*m.*	*used for recreational or sports activities*
9. 年轻人	niánqīngrén	*n.*	young people
10. 懂	dǒng	*v.*	to understand
11. 听说	tīngshuō	*v.*	(I) heard (that)
12. 逐渐	zhújiàn	*adv.*	gradually
13. 各种各样	gèzhǒng gèyàng		various; all kinds of
14. 脸谱	liǎnpǔ	*n.*	types of facial makeup in Peking operas
15. 武打	wǔdǎ	*n.*	acrobatic fighting in Chinese opera or dance

Notes

1. "你买到票了吗？"

   到 is a verb, serving as a complement of the main verb 买 in this sentence, indicating the result of 买 .

   他见到老师了吗?

   那本书我已经找到了。

   The negative form of "verb + '到'" is 没 or 没有 put before the verb.

   他没有见到老师。

51

那本书我没找到。

2. "虽然售票处没有票了，但是一定会有人来退票。"

　　"虽然……但是……" is a pair of conjunctions showing adversative relation, indicating that things will present an opposite state or have an opposite result given certain conditions.

　　虽然他生病了，但是还坚持工作。

　　虽然这件衣服很贵，但是质量并不太好。

Exercise

On your own

Match the left and right columns according to the text.

(1) 虽然售票处没有票了　　　　就进电影院。

(2) 杰克一买到票　　　　越来越多了。

(3) 虽然马明看不懂京剧　　　　但是一定会有人来退票。

(4) 现在喜欢京剧的年轻人　　　　但是他喜欢京剧的脸谱。

Conversation practice

Make dialogues with the complement of result according to the pictures.

A：米饭吃完了吗?

B：米饭吃完了。

Class activity & communication task

(1) Work in groups of three people. Act out a negotiation situation where there is disagreement of opinions. Raise personal views, explain your reasons, give short comment or sum up others' opinions. For example, when planning for weekend activities, some people hope to play soccer while others hope to watch movie. Explain reasons and comment on each other's reasons. Finally the groups work out solutions.

(2) Groups share their performance with the class.

Reading comprehension

古时候有个著名(zhùmíng, famous)的画家(huàjiā, painter)，有人请他在墙(qiáng, wall)上画四条龙。画完以后大家都说好，可是有个人发现这些龙没有眼睛。大家问画家，为什么不画眼睛。画家说，如果画了眼睛龙就活了，就会飞走(fēizǒu, to fly away)。大家不相信(xiāngxìn, to believe)，画家只好给两条龙画了眼睛。这时开始下雨，刮风，打雷(dǎléi, to thunder)。雨停了，大家再看，墙上只有两条龙了。

如果给故事加一个名字，应该是（ A ）

A. 画龙点睛(huàlóng-diǎnjīng)   B. 画虎类犬 (huàhǔ-lèiquǎn)

C. 画蛇添足 (huàshé-tiānzú)   C. 画饼充饥(huàbǐng-chōngjī)

Listen and practice

1. Listening comprehension

(1) Decide whether the following statements are true or false after listening to the recording.

① 杰克和美云一起去看京剧。(X)

② 现在喜欢京剧的年轻人不多，因为他们看不懂。(X)

③ 他们去晚了，没有买到票，所以他们没有看京剧。(T)

④ 年轻人喜欢看京剧的脸谱、武打，还有音乐。(T)

(2) Answer the following questions after listening to the recording.

Key words:

地方戏 dìfāngxì (local opera)　　川剧 chuānjù (Sichuan Opera)

变脸 biànliǎn (face-changing)　　剧种 jùzhǒng (operas)　　变换 biànhuàn (to change)

难道 nándào (an adverbial used for rhetorical questions)　　魔术 móshù (magic)

Questions:

① 中国四川的地方戏叫什么?

② 这个剧种最奇妙的技艺是什么?

③ 为什么说它很奇妙?

④ 你猜这种技艺的关键是什么?

2. Read the following tongue twister.

男 演 员 女 演 员,
nán yǎn yuán nǚ yǎn yuán

同 台 演 戏 说 方 言。
tóng tái yǎn xì shuō fāng yán

男 演 员 说 吴 方 言,
nán yǎn yuán shuō wú fāng yán

女 演 员 说 闽 方 言。
nǚ yǎn yuán shuō mǐn fāng yán

男 演 员 演 飞 行 员,
nán yǎn yuán yǎn fēi xíng yuán

女 演 员 演 研 究 员。
nǚ yǎn yuán yǎn yán jiū yuán

吴 方 言、 闽 方 言、 飞 行 员、 研 究 员,
wú fāng yán　mǐn fāng yán　fēi xíng yuán　yán jiū yuán

你 说 男 女 演 员 演 得 全 不 全?
nǐ shuō nán nǚ yǎn yuán yǎn de quán bu quán

> An actor and an actress, acting and speaking dialects together on stage.
> The actor speaks Wu dialect, the actress speaks Min dialect.
> The actor plays a pilot, the actress plays a researcher.
> Wu dialect, Min dialect, pilot, researcher ...
> What do you think of their roles?

Chinese characters

Write down the words related to moods or feelings.

笑哈哈　　　　生气 shēng qì ✓（笑眯眯）　　　　笑眯眯
　　　　　　　　　　　　　　　哭

Chinese culture

Peking Opera Facial Masks

The Peking Opera represents the best of Chinese traditional culture. Facial masks are the facial makeup of Peking Opera performers. The makeup method, unique in China, adopts certain colors and style based on the personality, temperament or types of characters. For example, Guan Yu's red facial mask shows loyalty, courage and righteousness. Zhang Fei's black facial mask shows integrity, courage and even recklessness. Dian Wei's yellow facial mask shows brutality and ferocity. Dou Erdun's blue or green facial mask shows a bold and a hot temper. Cao Cao's white facial mask generally shows a treacherous official and an evildoer.

6 昨晚我只睡(shuì)了四个小时

Getting started

What type of movies do you like to watch?

- 武打片
  kung fu movies
- 科幻片
  science fiction movies
- 爱情片
  romance movies
- 卡通片
  cartoons

- 警匪片
  police movies
- 恐怖片
  horror movies
- 惊险片
  thrillers
- 西部牛仔片
  Westerns

Text 1

Ma Ming is bending over the desk, sleeping. Meiyun is asking why.

美云： 马明，别睡了，就要上课了。

马明： 对不起，我又累 (lèi) 又困 (kùn)，昨天 (zuótiān) 晚上我只睡了四个小时 (xiǎoshí)。

美云： 你睡得太少 (shǎo) 了。昨天晚上你干什么了？

马明： 我写 (xiě) 作文 (zuòwén) 写了三个小时，然后又看了两个小时电视。

美云： 什么电视？

马明： 武打片 (wǔdǎpiàn)。是一个香港明星 (míngxīng) 演 (yǎn) 的。他演得好极 (jí) 了。

美云： 他叫什么名字？

马明： 他叫什么龙，我忘了。

美云： 是李小龙 (Lǐ Xiǎolóng) 还是成龙 (Chéng Lóng)？

马明： 对了，是成龙。

Text 2

Meiyun is telling her mum about one of the musical instrument performances given by Jack.

上(shàng)周末(zhōumò)学校举行音乐会，我的朋友杰克演奏(yǎnzòu)了中国的小提琴(xiǎotíqín)曲(qǔ)《梁祝》(Liángzhù)。他拉(lā)得好极了。他的演奏一结束，大家就鼓起掌(gǔ...zhǎng)来①。杰克六岁就开始学习小提琴，他已经学了十年了。不过，我是第一次(dì...cì)听他演奏中国乐曲。听说，学习小提琴以前，他还学了两年钢琴(gāngqín)呢。

---

① 鼓起掌来：begin to applaud

New words

1. 睡	shuì	v.	to sleep
2. 累	lèi	adj.	tired
3. 困	kùn	adj.	sleepy
4. 昨天	zuótiān	n.	yesterday
5. 小时	xiǎoshí	n.	hour
6. 少	shǎo	adj.	little; few; less
7. 写	xiě	v.	to write
8. 作文	zuòwén	n.	composition
9. 武打片	wǔdǎpiàn	n.	kung fu movie
10. 明星	míngxīng	n.	star (a famous performer)
11. 演	yǎn	v.	to play; to perform; to act
12. 极	jí	adv.	extremely; to the greatest extent; exceedingly
13. 上 (个)	shàng (gè)	n.	last; most recent
14. 周末	zhōumò	n.	weekend
15. 演奏	yǎnzòu	v.	to play (a musical instrument)
16. 小提琴	xiǎotíqín	n.	violin
17. (乐) 曲	(yuè) qǔ	n.	tune; musical composition
18. 拉 (琴)	lā (qín)	v.	to play (certain musical instruments, such as violin, accordion)
19. 鼓掌	gǔzhǎng	v.	to applaud
20. 第……次	dì...cì		the ... time (第 used before numerals to form ordinal numbers)
21. 钢琴	gāngqín	n.	piano

Proper nouns

1. 李小龙	Lǐ Xiǎolóng	Bruce Lee
2. 成龙	Chéng Lóng	Jackie Chan
3. 《梁祝》	Liángzhù	*Butterfly Lovers*

59

1. "昨天晚上我只睡了四个小时。"

   "Quantity word + time word", as a complement after the verb, shows the duration of the action or the continuation of the state. This sentence means Ma Ming had a very short sleep.

   我们准备锻炼十分钟。

   他打算在中国学习五年。

   The verb with complement of duration may be followed by aspect particles 了 and 过, but mustn't be followed by 着.

   昨晚我只睡了四个小时。

   他在中国学习过五年。

2. "他演得好极了。"

   The structure "Adjective + '极了'" is often used in Chinese to indicate a high degree.

   风景美极了。

   这里的人多极了。

3. "他的演奏一结束，大家就鼓起掌来。"

   As a directional verb put after the verb, 起来 may indicate different meanings. It indicates the beginning and continuation of the action in this sentence. When there is an object after the verb, the object is generally put in between 起 and 来.

   鼓掌, as a separable word, has a structure of "Verb + Object". Therefore 鼓掌 and 起来 should both be used separately. Generally, all combinations of separable words and 起来 need to follow this structure.

   说起话来　　　游起泳来　　　唱起歌来

Exercise

On your own

Rearrange the following words and phrases according to the texts and then write their numbers in the phoenix's tail to make a complete sentence.

(1) 昨天晚上①　四个小时②　只睡了③　马明④

(2) 三个小时①　写作业(homework)②　写③　了④　马明⑤

(3) 歌①　他②　高兴地③　唱④　起⑤　来⑥

Conversation practice

Match the left and right columns first and then finish the conversation and practice with your partner.

玩了八个小时电脑　　脚很疼
踢了三个小时足球　　手很疼
写了三个小时汉字　　眼睛很疼

A：你怎么了？
B：我的 <u>眼睛很疼</u> 。昨天我 <u>玩了八个小时电脑</u>。
A：需要我帮忙吗？
B：不用了，多谢！（太好了，谢谢你！）

Class activity & communication task

(1) Read the following information about personal hobbies.
(2) Work in groups of three classmates. Ask about classmates' hobbies, and note down their experience.
(3) Groups share their reports with the class. Explain the reasons of the hobbies, describe relevant experience or tell stories.

艺术与爱好

　　现在，越来越多的小学生、中学生学习艺术，有的学绘画，有的学音乐、乐器，有的学舞蹈……

　　杨华，女，高中二年级学生。从小喜欢音乐，从6岁开始学习小提琴。虽然现在学习很忙，但每个星期天下午她总是拉两个小时的小提琴：

"拉琴时，我的心里只有音乐，我觉得快乐极了，这是最好的<u>休息</u>……"

　　李云迪，男，5岁时<u>获得</u>四川省儿童手风琴比赛第一名，12岁第一次参加国际钢琴<u>比赛</u>，<u>获得</u>Stravinsky 青少年<u>国际钢琴比赛</u>B组第三名。2000年，获得第十四届Chopin国际钢琴比赛金奖。大家都认为他的钢琴弹得好极了。

Listen and practice

Listening comprehension

(1) Decide whether the following statements are true or false after listening to the recording.

Key words:

周末 zhōumò (weekend)　　　　　非洲 Fēizhōu (Africa)

True or false:

① 学习中国乐曲以前，他还学习了非洲乐曲呢。(T)

② 杰克四岁就开始学习小提琴。(F)

③ 他已经学了十二年音乐了。(T)

④ 在音乐会上，杰克演奏的小提琴曲最好。(F)

⑤ 这是杰克第一次在音乐会上演奏乐曲。(F)

⑥ 他的演奏一结束，大家就鼓起掌来。(T)

(2) Answer the following questions after listening to the recording.

Key words:

魔术师 móshùshī (magician)　　　　设计 shèjì (to design)

魔术 móshù (magic)　　　　　　　表演 biǎoyǎn (to perform)

需要 xūyào (need)　　　　　　　　观众 guānzhòng (audience)

邀请 yāoqǐng (to invite)

Questions:

① 魔术师的新魔术需要谁的帮助？

② 魔术师为什么让儿子和观众坐在一起？

③ 魔术师为什么对观众说他不认识这个孩子？

④ 孩子有没有告诉观众他是谁？

Chinese characters

Write down the types of films according to the hints.

Hints			Films
1.	李小龙 Bruce Lee	武术 wushu	功夫 gongfu	武打片
2.	警察 police	罪犯 criminal	枪战 gunfight	警匪片
3.	泰坦尼克号 Titanic	甜蜜 sweet	感动 move	爱情片
4.	害怕 fear	紧张 nervous	黑暗 dark	恐怖片

Listen and practice

Read and sing

青 春 舞 曲
qīng chūn wǔ qǔ

太 阳 下 山 明 早 依 旧 爬 上 来，
tài yáng xià shān míng zǎo yī jiù pá shàng lái

花 儿 谢 了 明 年 还 是 一 样 的 开。
huā ér xiè le míng nián hái shi yí yàng de kāi

美 丽 小 鸟 飞 去 无 踪 影，
měi lì xiǎo niǎo fēi qù wú zōng yǐng

我 的 青 春 小 鸟 一 样 不 回 来。
wǒ de qīng chūn xiǎo niǎo yí yàng bù huí lái

Dance Music of Youth

The sun will rise again after it sets,

The flower will bloom again after it withers.

Pretty birds have flown away, nowhere be found,

My youth has faded away and never come back again.

青春舞曲

新 疆 民 歌
吴文胜编曲

太阳下山明早依旧爬 上 来，　　花儿谢了明年还是一 样的开。

美丽小鸟飞 去 无 踪 影，　　我的青春小鸟一样不 回 来，

我的青春小鸟一样不 回 来。　　别得那呀哟，　　别得那呀哟！

我的青春小鸟一样不 回 来。　　别得那呀哟，　　别得那呀哟！

我的青春小鸟一样不 回 来。

UNIT SUMMARY

FUNCTIONAL USAGE

1. Find out information

你 到 哪 儿 去 了 ？
nǐ dào nǎr qù le

2. Discuss solutions

没 有 退 票 怎 么 办 ？
méi yǒu tuì piào zěn me bàn

那 怎 么 办 ？
nà zěn me bàn

3. Give a brief description

去 年 他 到 中 国 去 了 ， 他 在 北 京 学 习 了 一 年 呢 。
qù nián tā dào zhōng guó qù le tā zài běi jīng xué xí le yì nián ne

杰 克 六 岁 就 开 始 学 习 小 提 琴 ， 他 已 经 学 了
jié kè liù suì jiù kāi shǐ xué xí xiǎo tí qín tā yǐ jīng xué le

十 年 了 。
shí nián le

4. Give a brief comment

虽 然 我 看 不 懂 京 剧 ， 但 是 我 喜 欢 看 各
suī rán wǒ kàn bù dǒng jīng jù dàn shì wǒ xǐ huan kàn gè

种 各 样 的 脸 谱 和 武 打 。
zhǒng gè yàng de liǎn pǔ hé wǔ dǎ

GRAMMAR FOCUS

Sentence pattern   *Example*

1. 简单趋向补语

我 也 想 到 中 国 去。
wǒ yě xiǎng dào zhōng guó qù

2. 副词 "差点儿"

我 差 点 儿 不 认 识 他 了。
wǒ chà diǎnr bú rèn shi tā le

3. 重动句 "动宾结构 + 动词 + 得"

他 说 汉 语 说 得 非 常 好。
tā shuō hàn yǔ shuō de fēi cháng hǎo

4. 动词 + "到"

你 买 到 票 了 吗?
nǐ mǎi dào piào le ma

5. "虽然……但是……"

虽 然 售 票 处 没 有 票
suī rán shòu piào chù méi yǒu piào

了, 但 是 一 定 会 有 人
le dàn shì yí dìng huì yǒu rén

来 退 票。
lái tuì piào

6. 形容词 + "极了"

他 拉 得 好 极 了。
tā lā de hǎo jí le

7. 动词 + "起" + 宾语 + "来"

大 家 就 鼓 起 掌 来。
dà jiā jiù gǔ qǐ zhǎng lái

8. 动词 + 时量补语

昨 天 晚 上 我 只 睡 了
zuó tiān wǎn shàng wǒ zhǐ shuì le

四 个 小 时。
sì gè xiǎo shí

CHINESE CHARACTERS REVIEW

汉字 Chinese character		拼音 *Pinyin*	词语组合 Language composition	
慕	莫心	mù	美慕	爱慕
(想)	相心	xiǎng	想念	想象
胜	月生	shèng	名胜	胜利
票	西示	piào	车票	售票处
说	讠兑	shuō	说话	听说
睡	目垂	shuì	睡觉	睡眠
写	一与	xiě	写字	写作业
忘	亡心	wàng	忘记	难忘
演	氵寅	yǎn	演员	演出
奏	夫天	zòu	演奏	奏乐
视	礻见	shì	电视	近视
钢	钅冈	gāng	钢琴	钢笔

Unit Three

Two Generations

7 我很烦(fán)

Getting started

Describe what people are doing in the pictures by using the following words.

叫……起床

(to wake somebody up)

很晚回家

(to come back home very late)

听音乐

(to listen to the music)

拿走……的耳机

(to take away one's headphones)

psychological counseling

张大夫 (Zhāng dàifu)，哈佛大学毕业(Hāfó Dàxué bìyè)，专门研究(zhuānmén yánjiū)青少年(qīngshàonián)和父母(fùmǔ)的关系问题。欢迎您来作心理咨询(xīnlǐ zīxún)。电话：995-6653。

Text 1

Mum is asking Ma Ming why he came home so late.

妈妈： 小明 (Xiǎomíng)，今天你是不是很晚才回来？

马明： 不晚，现在刚六点，我四点五十就到家了。

妈妈： 学校不是三点就放学 (fàngxué) 了吗？

马明： 我和几 (jǐ) 个同学在教室听音乐。我们四点半才离开 (líkāi) 学校。

妈妈： 你最近回家越来越晚了。做完作业 (zuòyè) 了吗？

马明： 还没有。我修 (xiū) 好滑板再做。

妈妈： 你应该做完作业再做别的事情 (shìqing)。晚上你还要去中文学校呢。

马明： 别的同学都在玩，可是你总是让我学习 (xuéxí)、学习、学习！

70

Text 2

Jack is complaining about something to Ma Ming.

我很烦，爸爸越来越不理解(lǐjiě)我了。星期天(xīngqītiān)早晨，我九点就起床了，可是爸爸还批评(pīpíng)我："你怎么九点才起床，又睡懒觉(shuì lǎnjiào)！"每天下午，我不到六点就回家了，可是他问："你怎么这么晚才回来？"我喜欢一边写作业，一边听音乐，可是他一看见就批评我，还拿走(zǒu)我的耳机(ěrjī)。让我更生气(shēngqì)的是妈妈的态度(tàidù)。每次爸爸批评我，她都说："你爸爸说得对。"

New words

1. 烦	fán	*adj.*	vexed; annoyed; irritated
2. 放学	fàngxué	*v.*	(school) to let out; (of classes) to be over
3. 几	jǐ	*approx. num.*	a few; several; some
4. 离开	líkāi	*v.*	to leave
5. 作业	zuòyè	*n.*	homework
6. 修	xiū	*v.*	to repair; to fix
7. 事情	shìqing	*n.*	thing; matter; business; affair
8. 学习	xuéxí	*v.*	to study
9. 理解	lǐjiě	*v.*	to understand
10. 星期天	xīngqītiān	*n.*	Sunday
11. 批评	pīpíng	*v.*	to criticize
12. 睡懒觉	shuì lǎnjiào		to sleep in; to get up late
13. 走	zǒu	*v.*	to leave; to go/take away
14. 耳机	ěrjī	*n.*	headphones
15. 生气	shēngqì	*v.*	to get angry
16. 态度	tàidù	*n.*	attitude

Proper noun

小明	Xiǎomíng	Xiaoming

Notes

1. "现在刚六点。"

   The adverb 刚 in this sentence, put before quantity word indicating time, shows something happens exactly at this point, neither early nor late.

   我们刚学完第一课。

   他刚毕业。

   电影刚结束。

2. "我四点五十就到家了。"

   The adverb 就 in this sentence, put before verb, shows that the speaker thinks the action or event takes place early or finishes early.

老张二十岁就结婚了。（说话人认为二十岁结婚很早。）

音乐会十点钟就结束了。（结束的时间比说话人预想得早。）

3. "你最近回家越来越晚了。／ 爸爸越来越不理解我了。"

The structure "'越来越' + Adjective/Verb" is generally used to show the degree goes deeper as time passes. The structure can serve as a predicate, attribute or a complement in the sentence.

他的汉语水平越来越高。（谓语）

越来越多的人喜欢这里了。（定语）

这个城市变得越来越漂亮。（补语）

Exercise

On your own

1. Describe the following pictures using 越来越 .

(1) 走来走 胖。

(2) 她越走 赶。

(3) 他走来走 téng 疼

(4) 你走来走 大。

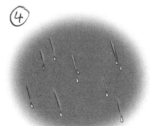

2. Make a sentence with 就 or 才 according to each picture.

①

妈妈六点半就起床了。

②

爸爸九点才起床。

③

美云七点半才出门。

④

美华四点才回家。

3. Make complaints based on the pictures.

①

②

③

Conversation practice

1. Number the following pictures and then read the story.

A.

B.

C.

D.

The correct order is: (1) pic___D___ (2) pic___B___ (3) pic___A___ (4) pic___C___

2. Complete the conversation based on the pictures and given clues. Imagine more situations and practice conversation with your partner.

A：你起床了吗?

B：我刚走来_____。(刚)

75

A：你为什么这么生气?

B：_____。(刚)

Class activity & communication task

(1) Complete the chart below.

这样的孩子是好孩子吗?		这样的父母是好父母吗?	
学习成绩①好	☑	经常给孩子买玩具	☒
喜欢运动	☑	给孩子很多零花钱	☒
喜欢艺术	☑	经常和孩子商量	☑
喜欢独立②思考	☑	经常和孩子一起玩	☑
放学后马上回家	☑	不看孩子的信、日记④	☑
不跟异性③同学多说话	☑	决定孩子买什么衣服	☒
做什么事情都告诉父母	☑	告诉孩子应该学什么	☒
认真完成老师布置的任务	☑	不允许孩子和异性在一起	☒
……		……	

(2) Ask your classmates questions based on the sentences in the above chart. Find out the standards of a good kid or good parents.

(3) Give a presentation of A Good Kid or Good Parents to your class.

---

① 成绩：grades
② 独立：independent
③ 异性：the opposite sex
④ 日记：diary

Listen and practice

1. Listening comprehension

   (1) Decide whether the following statements are true or false after listening to the recording.

   Key words:

   互相理解 hùxiāng lǐjiě (to understand each other)

   放学 fàngxué ((school) to let out)　认为 rènwéi (to think / believe)

   觉得 juéde (to feel)　　　　　　　累 lèi (tired)

   True or false:

   ① 马明每天放学以后七点回家。(✗) ✓

   ② 马明的妈妈觉得他每天回家太晚了。(✓) ✓

   ③ 马明星期天早晨九点起床，妈妈觉得他起得很早。(✗) ✓

   ④ 马明觉得他和妈妈越来越不能互相理解了。(✓) ✓

   ⑤ 马明觉得一边做作业一边听音乐不累。(✓) ✓

   ⑥ 他妈妈一看见他听音乐就拿走他的耳机。(✓) ✓

   (2) Answer the following questions after listening to the recording.

   Key words:

   南京 Nánjīng (Nanjing)　　三分之二 sān fēn zhī èr (two thirds)

   三分之一 sān fēn zhī yī (one third)　　压力 yālì (pressure)

   成绩 chéngjì (performance)　却 què (but)　　不敢 bùgǎn (dare not)

   Questions:

   ① 这段材料是对什么人做的调查？

   ② 有多少人感到快乐？有多少人感到不快乐？

   ③ 不快乐的原因是什么？

   ④ 你快乐吗？为什么？

2. Read the following ancient poem.

月　落　乌　啼　霜　满　天，
yuè　luò　wū　tí　shuāng mǎn　tiān

江　枫　渔　火　对　愁　眠。
jiāng fēng　yú　huǒ　duì　chóu mián

姑　苏　城　外　寒　山　寺，
gū　sū　chéng wài　hán　shān　sì

夜　半　钟　声　到　客　船。
yè　bàn zhōng shēng dào　kè　chuán

（唐·张继《枫桥夜泊》）

Moon's down, crows cry and frosts fills all the sky;

By maples and boat lights, I sleeplessly lie.

Outside Gusu Cold-Hill Temple's in sight;

Its ringing bells reach my boat at midnight.

Chinese characters

Write Chinese characters as required.

(1) Write four characters with a final "an".

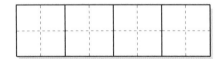

(2) Write four characters with "氵".

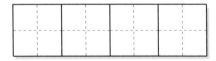

(3) Write four characters with an up-down structure.

Tiger Mother

The word "tiger mother" comes from the book *The Battle Hymn of the Tiger Mother* written by an American Chinese mother Amy Chua in 2011. The book tells the story of how the mother adopts a very rigorous method in educating her two daughters, forcing them to study what their parents tell them to study, and finally proves to be successful.

"Tiger mother" in fact represents a very rigorous Chinese way of education. Tiger mother's style is very popular in China where most children are the only ones in their families. Originated in the traditional Chinese way focusing on knowledge teaching and rote learning, the tiger mother's style is very different from western concept which emphasizing respecting children's personality and free development. Although she is successful, those against her think she is almost a children abuser. What do you think?

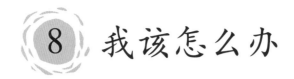

8 我该怎么办

Getting started

Discuss: What do you usually do on weekends? What do your parents think of the way you spend your weekend?

去野餐，送饭，跟朋友约会……

当服务员，参加舞会，当保姆……

Text 1

Meiyun is on the phone with her mother. She is asking her mother if she can sleep over the night at her classmate's home.

美云：喂，妈妈，我是美云。

妈妈：美云，你在哪儿？现在已经十一点了。

美云：别担心①(dānxīn)，妈妈，我在同学家，一个同学过生日。我不是告诉过您了吗？

妈妈：你打算几点回家？

美云：再过一个小时，行吗？

妈妈：现在已经很晚了……

美云：妈妈，我能不能住在同学家？

妈妈：那不行！

美云：妈妈，求(qiú)求您②！同学们都在这儿，我不想现在自己回家。

妈妈：这样(zhèyàng)吧，一个小时以后我和你爸爸去接(jiē)你。

---

① 别担心：Don't worry

② 求求您：please...; I beg you...

Text 2

Meiyun's mother's worries.

我有两个孩子，老(lǎo)大是女儿，今年16岁。她比以前高了，也比以前漂亮了，可是没有以前听话(tīnghuà)了。她不再喜欢我给她买的衣服了①。她总是对我说"这个没有那个时髦，这件没有那件漂亮"什么的②。星期六，她常常很晚才回家，有时候她还要求(yāoqiú)在同学家过夜(guòyè)。我想知道她有些(yǒuxiē)什么样的朋友，可是她对我保密(bǎomì)。她每次打电话，都躲(duǒ)在房间里。我越来越不了解(liǎojiě)她了。你们说，我该怎么办？

---

① 不再……了：no more...; no longer...

② ……什么的：(used after a series of items) things like that; and so on; and what not

New words

1. 担心	dānxīn	*v.*	to worry
2. 求	qiú	*v.*	to plead; to beg; to request
3. 这样 (吧)	zhèyàng (ba)	*pron.*	like this; so; this way
4. 接	jiē	*v.*	to meet (sb)；to pick sb up
5. 老	lǎo	*prefix*	*used before the noun, adjective, numeral*
6. 听话	tīnghuà	*adj.*	obedient; heed what an elder or superior says
7. 要求	yáoqiú	*v.*	to ask; to demand; to request
8. 过夜	guòyè	*v.*	to sleep over; to put up for the night
9. 有些	yǒuxiē	*pron.*	some; a few
10. 保密	bǎomì	*v.*	to keep sth. secret; to maintain secrecy
11. 躲	duǒ	*v.*	to hide
12. 了解	liǎojiě	*v.*	to understand; to know

Notes

1. "我不是告诉过您了吗？"

The pattern "不是……吗" can be used in Chinese as an emphasis. The role of the sentence is to emphasize and affirm the fact "我告诉过你".

你不是说一定参加吗？

他们不是去看电影了吗？

这里的夏天不是很凉快吗？

2. "再过一个小时，行吗？"

The adverb 再 in this sentence, put before the verb 过 , shows the continuation of the action.

再过半年，这条路就修好了。

咱们再玩一会儿吧。

3. "她总是对我说……什么的。"

The pronoun 什么的 may refer to anything. Normally used after one part or several coordinative parts, 什么的 has the same meaning as 等等 and is more popular in spoken Chinese.

> 桌子上放着笔、本子什么的。
>
> 他给了孩子一些饼干、糖果什么的。
>
> 妈妈总是让我一回家就做作业、读中文什么的。

4. "老大是女儿。"

Used before the number, the prefix 老 in this sentence shows the seniority among brothers and sisters, for example 老二 and 老三 . But the oldest is called 老大 instead of 老一 .

> 我家有两个孩子，老大是女孩，老二是男孩。

Exercise

On your own

Use 什么的 to describe the pictures.

Conversation practice

1. Complete the conversation using "在 + Verb". Practice with your partner.

(1)　A：这本书怎么样?

　　　B：太好看了，我想 _____ 。

(2)　A：我们什么时候下课?

　　　B：快了，_____ 。

(3)　A：妈妈我不想吃了。

　　　B：不行，_____ 。

2. Please match the dialogue with the picture and then practice with your partner. In pairs practice expressing requests, approval and denials.

(1) A：爸爸，我和我们班同学一起去海边玩，求您了，让我去吧！

B：我不是告诉过你了吗？老师不参加，你就不能去。

(2) A：喂。

B：喂，你好。

A：妈妈，今天晚上我晚一点儿回家，行吗？我想去同学家玩。

B：行，你十一点半以前到家吧。

(3) A：我很想参加这个晚会，求您了，让我去吧！

B：我不是告诉过你了吗？不可以太晚回家。

A：老师也在。

B：那好吧，不过你必须十二点以前到家。

Class activity & communication task

(1) Work in groups of three people. Design a conversation. Two classmates act out the conversation where one classmate makes the invitation, the second classmate refuses and explains why, and the third classmate briefly introduces the situation and makes comment on the reasons of refusal.

(2) Share your group performance with the class. Find out the best situation design and the most persuasive reasons.

Reading comprehension

Sign

　　唉，再过半个小时就十二点了，老大怎么还是没有回到家呢？这孩子，总是这么晚回家，我怎么能不担心她呢？我是不是给她打个电话？可是她最烦我打电话催她。天下做父母的不容易啊！

True or false:

① 现在是 12：30 。 (F)

② 老大是一个女孩子。(T)

③ 妈妈打过电话催老大回家。(T)

Listen and practice

1. Listening comprehension

   (1) Decide whether the following statements are true or false after listening to the recording.

   Key words:

   小孩子 xiǎoháizi (little kid)　　　　　总是 zǒngshì (always)

   以前 yǐqián (before; in the past)　　　小女孩儿 xiǎo nǚháir (little girl)

   True or false:

   ① 我妈妈觉得我是个小孩子。(T) ✓

   ② 我妈妈给我买的衣服很时髦。(F) ✓

   ③ 我妈妈不喜欢我自己买的衣服。(T) ✓

   ④ 星期六，我要求在同学家过夜，我妈妈同意了。(F) ✓

   ⑤ 我妈妈想知道我的朋友是什么人。(F) x T

   ⑥ 我在房间里打电话，因为不想让我妈听见。(T) ✓

   (2) Answer the following questions after listening to the recording.

   Key words:

类型 lèixíng (type)	严厉 yánlì (severe, stern)	严格 yángé (strict)
管理 guǎnlǐ (management)	放养 fàngyǎng (to raise children in a lax way)	
管 guǎn (to control)	满足 mǎnzú (to satisfy)	聊天儿 liáotiānr (to chat) ✓
尊重 zūnzhòng (to respect)	建议 jiànyì (suggestion)	

Questions:

① "严厉型"教育是怎样的? 孩子什么 dōu 的 ting 父母 的。✓

② "放养型"教育是怎样的? 不 guǎn 孩子。

③ "朋友型"教育是怎样的? gēn 孩 聊天儿。

④ 你的父母采用哪种教育方法? 我的妈妈 是 tiger 妈妈。

2. Read the following modern poem.

妈　妈，请　放　开　你
mā ma qǐng fàng kāi nǐ

春　天　一　样　温　暖　的　手，
chūn tiān yí yàng wēn nuǎn de shǒu

让　我　独　个　儿　在　坎　坷　的　路　上
ràng wǒ dú gèr　 zài kǎn kě de lù shang

磕　磕　碰　碰　向　前　走。
kē　 kē pèng pèng xiàng qián zǒu

妈　妈，亲　爱　的　妈　妈，
mā ma qīn ài de mā ma

请　松　开　你　慈　爱　的　手，
qǐng sōng kāi nǐ cí ài de shǒu

让　我　踩　着　坚　实　的　土　地，
ràng wǒ cǎi zhe jiān shí de tǔ dì

跟　困　难　和　胜　利　交　朋　友。
gēn kùn nan hé shèng lì jiāo péng you

Mom, please let go your hand as warm as spring,

let me, on the bumpy road,

walk ahead conquering hardships,

Mom, dear Mom,

please release your affectionate hand,

let me step on the solid earth,

and make friends with hardships and victory.

Chinese character

Radical-matching. Please choose one radical from the T-shirt and skirt respectively which can form a new character, and then write it down in the table.

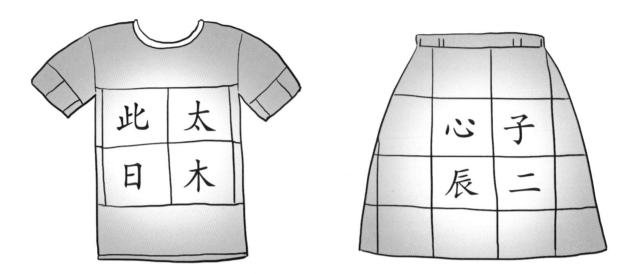

结构	此＋二		
整字	些		

9 望子成龙(wàngzǐ-chénglóng)

Getting started

What expectations do your parents have for your future?

Text 1

Meihua complains to Meiyun about his quarrel with mom.

美云：美华，怎么生气了？

美华：刚才和妈妈吵架(chǎojià)了。

美云：怎么回事？

美华：我四点半一到家，妈妈就让我写汉字(Hànzì)、读(dú)古诗(gǔshī)，我想玩会儿电脑，和网友(wǎngyǒu)聊聊天儿，都不行。

美云：妈妈是怕你把中文忘记了嘛。

美华：妈妈为什么不这样要求你？

美云：男孩儿(nánháir)和女孩儿不一样，我自己会安排(ānpái)，你总是玩。而且妈妈希望你以后像爸爸一样学国际(guójì)贸易(màoyì)专业(zhuānyè)，当然要更努力地学习啦。

美华：你说得不对，我也会自己安排时间，以后我要学电脑专业，玩电脑就是学习。

美云：你随便(suíbiàn)吧。

Text 2

Parents' hopes and children's hopes.

虽然父母(fùmǔ)都希望自已的孩子(háizi)健康(jiànkāng)，生活(shēnghuó)得幸福(xìngfú)，但是不同的父母对孩子会有不同的希望。

在中国，很多父母都希望孩子能继承(jìchéng)自已的事业(shìyè)，或者希望孩子去做父母想做可是没有机会(jīhuì)做的事情。例如(lìrú)：

电脑公司(gōngsī)的李先生说："我要让我儿子学习计算机(jìsuànjī)。"

餐馆的王太太说："我觉得知识越多越好，以前很想上(shàng)大学，可是没有机会。我希望我女儿将来上一个名牌(míngpái)大学。"

可是，孩子也有自已的想法，而且(érqiě)往往(wǎngwǎng)和父母的想法不一样。所以，也有的父母认为，应该让孩子做自已想做的事情。

你对这个问题怎么看？

New words

1. 望子成龙	wàngzǐ-chénglóng		to wish one's kid a great success in life
2. 吵架	chǎojià	*v.*	to quarrel
3. 汉字	Hànzì	*n.*	Chinese character
4. 读	dú	*v.*	to read
5. 古诗	gǔshī	*n.*	ancient poem
6. 网友	wǎngyǒu	*n.*	e-pals
7. 男孩儿	nánháir	*n.*	boy
8. 安排	ānpái	*v.*	to arrange
9. 国际	guójì	*n.*	international
10. 贸易	màoyì	*n.*	trade
11. 专业	zhuānyè	*n.*	major
12. 随便	suíbiàn	*v.*	to do at one's will
13. 父母	fùmǔ	*n.*	parents
14. 孩子	háizi	*n.*	child
15. 健康	jiànkāng	*adj.*	healthy
16. 生活	shēnghuó	*v.*	to live
17. 幸福	xìngfú	*adj.*	happy
18. 继承	jìchéng	*v.*	to carry on; to inherit
19. 事业	shìyè	*n.*	career
20. 机会	jīhuì	*n.*	chance; opportunity
21. 例如	lìrú	*v.*	for example; for instance
22. 公司	gōngsī	*n.*	company; firm
23. 计算机	jìsuànjī	*n.*	computer
24. 上（大学）	shàng (dàxué)	*v.*	to go (to university)
25. 名牌	míngpái	*n.*	prestigious/famous brand
26. 而且	érqiě	*conj.*	and that; in addition
27. 往往	wǎngwǎng	*adv.*	often

1. "……或者希望孩子去做父母想做可是没有机会做的事情。"

As a conjunction, 或者 in this sentence shows a choice.

问小张或者老李都可以。

Sometimes two 或者 can be used together.

或者你去，或者他去，反正必须有一个人去。

2. "我觉得知识越多越好"。

越 is an adverb. "越A越B" shows B changes in degree as A changes.

我越看越喜欢。

大家越讨论，问题解决得越好。

动物越小越可爱。

3. "……而且往往和父母的想法不一样。"

As an adverb, 往往 shows that something often happens.

那里是原始森林，往往走四五十千米都见不到人烟。

到底什么是最真实的，我们往往不知道。

Exercise

On your own

1. Rearrange the following words and phrases according to the texts and then write their numbers in the phoenix's tail to make a complete sentence.

(1) 很多父母①   或者②   去做③   父母想做的事情④

     孩子继承自己的事业⑤   希望⑥

(2) 才①   10岁②   会③   王太太的女儿④   系鞋带⑤

(3) 王太太的女儿①   就②   写汉字③   3岁④   开始⑤

(4) 看京剧①   晚上②   或者③   跟朋友④   聚会⑤

2. Complete the following sentences based on the words given.

孩子的想法 _____。（往往）

他们的饮食习惯不同，_____。（餐具）

现在中国的很多家庭 _____。（一个孩子）

父母 _____。（期望）

Conversation practice

Make a conversation with your partner based on the following questions. Give complete sentences in your answers.

(1) 你觉得什么越快越好？

(2) 你觉得什么越容易越好？

(3) 你觉得什么越少越好？

(4) 你觉得什么越多越好？

Class activity & communication task

(1) The teacher makes a list of expressions about three functions: having no choice, persuasion, and rejection.

(2) Work in groups of three to four students. Each draws a picture related to the above functions. For example, the student who chooses "having no choice" draws a facial expression. The student who chooses "persuasion" draws a relevant situation.

(3) Collect the pictures in your group and make a free combination. Make up a story using the expressions given by the teacher.

(4) Select a group representative to show your combination of pictures to the class and tell the story.

Read and discuss

父母的期望①与孩子的心理②

中国的父母对孩子的期望都比较高。比如，父母们往往希望孩子上名牌大学，他们想各种办法送孩子上重点中学，请老师辅导③孩子，为孩子决定将来的职业。

父母的期望会对孩子产生什么影响？父母的期望太高，会使孩子自卑④、紧张。因此，父母应该尊重⑤孩子的兴趣⑥爱好，与孩子一起商量⑦未来⑧的职业⑨。

Discuss:

① 你的父母对你有什么希望？有什么要求？

② 将来你想上哪个大学？学什么专业？

③ 你跟父母谈过自己的理想吗？

Listen and practice

Listening comprehension

(1) Decide whether the following statements are true or false after listening to the recording.

Key words:

教育 jiàoyù(   )   争吵 zhēngchǎo(   )   嫌 xián(   )

诉苦 sùkǔ(   )   理解 lǐjiě(   )

True or false:

① 美华有时和妈妈争吵。(   )

② 因为不喜欢吃妈妈做的饭和妈妈争吵。(   )

③ 他想放学以后玩一会儿再回家。(   )

④ 妈妈让他读古诗，不让他玩电脑。(   )

⑤ 姐姐很理解他。(   )

---

① 期望：hope; expectation
② 心理：mentality; psychology
③ 辅导：to give guidance to
④ 自卑：to feel oneself inferior
⑤ 尊重：to respect
⑥ 兴趣：interest
⑦ 商量：to consult; to talk over
⑧ 未来：future
⑨ 职业：occupation; profession

(2) Answer the following questions after listening to the recording.

Key words:

孔融 Kǒng Róng (Kong Rong)　拜访 bàifǎng (to pay a visit to)　大官 dàguān (senior official)

守门人 shǒuménrén (janitor)　亲戚 qīnqi (relatives)　　　老子 Lǎozǐ (Laozi)

未必 wèibì (not necessarily)　尴尬 gāngà (embarrassed)

Questions:

① 孔融去拜访姓什么的大官？

② 老子和孔子是什么关系？

③ 孔融说自己和李姓大官是什么关系？

④ 姓陈的人怎么评价孔融？

⑤ 听了孔融的回答，姓陈的人为什么生气？

Chinese characters

Check the dictionary. Write idioms related to the 12 zodiac animals.

_____　_____　_____　_____

望子成龙　_____　_____　_____

_____　_____　_____　_____

Listen and practice

Read the following ancient poem.

百　川　东　到　海，
bǎi chuān dōng dào hǎi

何　时　复　西　归？
hé　shí　fù　xī　guī

少　壮　不　努　力，
shào zhuàng bù　nǔ　lì

老　大　徒　伤　悲。
lǎo　dà　tú shāng bēi

（汉 ·《乐府诗集 · 长歌行》节选）

One hundred rivers moving east to sea, when will they ever westward turn again? If while we're young and strong we don't strive hard, when we're grown old, no use whining then!

Gaokao in China

Gaokao is an abbreviation for the "unified national entrance examination for enrollment of institutions of higher education". The current *Gaokao* system refers to that after 1977 and it mainly features "unified national" and "standardization in setting exam questions".

Having been in place for over 30 years, the *Gaokao* system has brought major and profound influence on all social aspects in China. In general, *Gaokao* has contributed to selecting talents in China where students from all over the country are able to enter universities through their hard work and thus realize their dream. But the drawbacks have also become apparent. Because of its vital importance in determining students' fate, *Gaokao* has in fact become the "baton" to lead China's primary school and middle school education, thus reducing China's education to an "exam-oriented education". For this reason, China is right now exploring all kinds of reforms on *Gaokao* and is advocating "quality-oriented education" instead.

UNIT SUMMARY

FUNCTIONAL USAGE

1. Complaining

我 很 烦！
wǒ hěn fán

你 总 是 让 我……
nǐ zǒng shì ràng wǒ

更 让 我 生 气 的 是……
gèng ràng wǒ shēng qì de shì

2. Requesting permission and refusing a request

妈 妈，求 求 您……
mā ma qiú qiu nín

那 不 行。
nà bù xíng

3. Enquiring and explaining reasons

怎 么 生 气 了？
zěn me shēng qì le

怎 么 回 事？
zěn me huí shì

我 觉 得……
wǒ jué de

……所 以……
suǒ yǐ

4. Refusal

妈 妈 为 什 么 不
mā ma wèi shén me bú

这 样 要 求 你。
zhè yàng yāo qiú nǐ

你 说 得 不 对。我
nǐ shuō de bú duì wǒ

也 会 自 己 安 排
yě huì zì jǐ ān pái

时 间。
shí jiān

5. Expressing having no choice

你 随 便 吧。
nǐ suí biàn ba

GRAMMAR FOCUS

Sentence pattern	*Example*
1. 副词 "刚"	现在刚六点。 xiàn zài gāng liù diǎn
2. 副词 "就"	我四点五十就到家了。 wǒ sì diǎn wǔ shí jiù dào jiā le
3. "越来越……"	爸爸越来越不理解我了。 bà ba yuè lái yuè bù lǐ jiě wǒ le
4. 反问句式 "不是……吗"	我不是告诉过您了吗? wǒ bú shì gào sù guo nín le ma
5. 副词 "再"	再过一个小时,行吗? zài guò yí gè xiǎo shí xíng ma
6. "……什么的"	她总是对我说……什么的。 tā zǒng shì duì wǒ shuō shén me de
7. 连词 "或者"	……或者希望孩子去做父 huò zhě xī wàng hái zi qù zuò fù 母想做可是没有机会做 mǔ xiǎng zuò kě shì méi yǒu jī huì zuò 的事情。 de shì qing
8. "越A越B"	知识越多越好。 zhī shi yuè duō yuè hǎo
9. 副词 "往往"	而且往往和父母的想法 ér qiě wǎng wǎng hé fù mǔ de xiǎng fǎ 不一样。 bù yí yàng

CHINESE CHARACTERS REVIEW

汉字 Chinese Character		拼音 *Pinyin*	词语组合 Language Composition
修	攸彡	xiū	修理　修改
理	王里	lǐ	理解　整理
解	角刀牛	jiě	理解　解决
批	扌比	pī	批评　批准
评	讠平	píng	批评　评论
懒	忄赖	lǎn	懒惰　睡懒觉
担	扌旦	dān	担心　担负
接	扌妾	jiē	接待　接受
躲	身朵	duǒ	躲避　躲开
健	亻建	jiàn	健康　健美
福	礻畐	fú	幸福　福气
例	亻列	lì	例子　举例
牌	片卑	pái	牌子　名牌
聊	耳卯	liáo	聊天　无聊
随	阝辶	suí	随便　随时

Unit Four

Different Cultures

Discuss the features of different cultures and the differences between them in a multi-cultural society.

10 婚礼的"颜色"

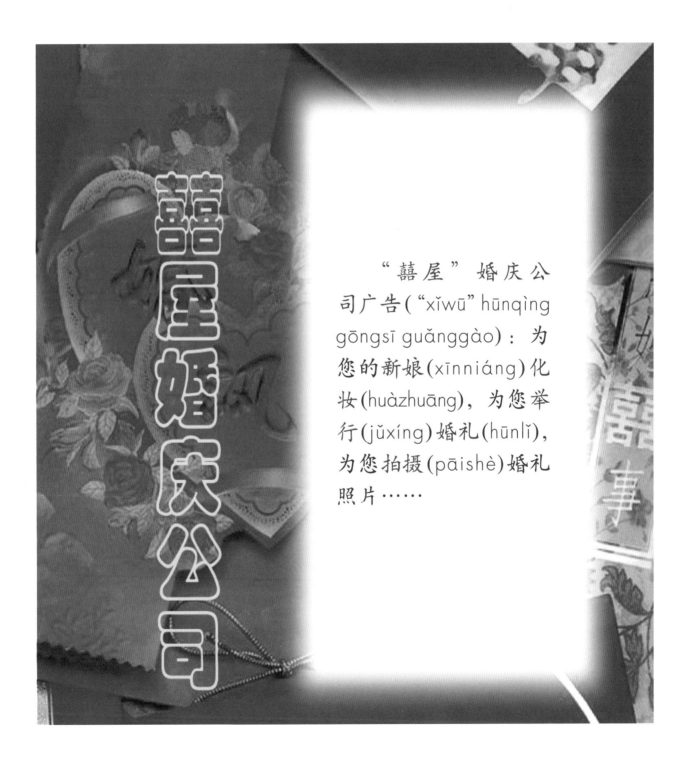

"囍屋"婚庆公司广告("xǐwū" hūnqìng gōngsī guǎnggào)：为您的新娘(xīnniáng)化妆(huàzhuāng)，为您举行(jǔxíng)婚礼(hūnlǐ)，为您拍摄(pāishè)婚礼照片……

Can you tell the differences between the two brides in the pictures by using the given words?

新娘 xīnniáng (bride)   漂亮 piàoliang (pretty)   红色 hóngsè (red)

白色 báisè (white)   穿 chuān (to wear)   旗袍 qípáo (cheongsam)

皮鞋 píxié (leather shoes)   花儿 huār (flower)   戴 dài (to wear)

Text 1

Jack and Meiyun are at Meiyun's uncle's wedding.

杰克：美云，今天这条街有多少人举行婚礼？

美云：不知道。怎么了？

杰克：你看，这边(zhèbiān)挂(guà)着红色的灯笼(dēnglong)。是不是在举行婚礼？

美云：哦，这是一家(jiā)饭馆，今天开张(kāizhāng)。

杰克：你看，那边(nàbiān)的门口也站着很多人。

美云：那就是我叔叔家。你听，鞭炮(biānpào)响(xiǎng)了，婚礼已经开始了。

杰克：中国人什么时候放(fàng)鞭炮？

美云：有喜事(xǐshì)的时候。挂灯笼、放鞭炮都是为了表示(biǎoshì)庆祝(qìngzhù)。过春节的时候，这里就更热闹了。

杰克：我应该对新郎(xīnláng)说什么？

美云：恭喜(gōngxǐ)恭喜。另外(lìngwài)，你也可以夸(kuā)夸他的新娘(xīnniáng)。

105

Text 2

Jack is talking about his impression of a Chinese wedding and comparing eastern and western weddings.

昨天我参加了美云叔叔的婚礼。新娘长得很漂亮。她身上(shēnshang)穿着红色的旗袍，脚(jiǎo)上是一双红色的皮鞋，头上还戴着一朵(duǒ)红色的花儿(huār)；房间里的很多东西都是红色的，墙(qiáng)上挂着红色的"囍"①字，桌子上摆(bǎi)着红色的蜡烛(làzhú)。这跟去年我阿姨(āyí)的婚礼很不一样。那天(nàtiān)我阿姨穿着白色的裙子，白色的皮鞋，戴着白色的花儿。如果说中国人的婚礼是红色的，那么是不是可以说，西方(xīfāng)人的婚礼是白色的呢？

---

① "囍", sticking to the wall when people hold their wedding ceremony means luck and happiness.

New words

1. 这边	zhèbiān	*pron.*	this side; here; this way
2. 挂	guà	*v.*	to hang
3. 灯笼	dēnglong	*n.*	lantern
4. 家	jiā	*m.*	*used for families or enterprises*
5. 开张	kāizhāng	*v.*	to open for business
6. 那边	nàbiān	*pron.*	that side; there
7. 鞭炮	biānpào	*n.*	firecracker
8. 响	xiǎng	*v.*	to bang; to make a sound
9. 放（鞭炮）	fàng (biānpào)	*v.*	to set off (firecrackers)
10. 喜事	xǐshì	*n.*	joyful event
11. 表示	biǎoshì	*v.*	to show; to express
12. 庆祝	qìngzhù	*n.*	celebration
13. 新郎	xīnláng	*n.*	bridegroom
14. 恭喜	gōngxǐ	*v.*	to congratulate
15. 另外	lìngwài	*n.*	in addition; besides
16. 夸	kuā	*v.*	to praise; to compliment
17. 新娘	xīnniáng	*n.*	bride
18. 身上	shēnshang	*n.*	on one's body
19. 脚	jiǎo	*n.*	foot
20. 朵	duǒ	*m.*	*used for flowers, clouds, etc.*
21. 花儿	huār	*n.*	flower
22. 墙	qiáng	*n.*	wall
23. 摆	bǎi	*v.*	to put; to place; to arrange
24. 蜡烛	làzhú	*n.*	candle
25. 阿姨	āyí	*n.*	aunt
26. 那天	nàtiān		on that day
27. 西方	xīfāng	*n.*	west

1. "这边挂着红色的灯笼。"

Existential sentences are used in Chinese to indicate the existence of something. The structure of an existential sentence is as such: "Location Noun + Verb + Noun". We discussed another kind of existential sentence in Lesson 30 of Book One: the 有 sentence indicating existence.

Quite a few existential sentences appeared in this lesson, such as "那边的门口也站着很多人""墙上挂着红色的'囍'字"and "桌子上摆着红色的蜡烛".

桌子上有一本书。

窗外是一片草地。

马路边停着一辆车。

2. "另外，你也可以夸夸他的新娘。"

Some verbs can be duplicated in Chinese, for example 夸夸 in the text. Duplicated verbs show a short duration of actions or actions performal in a relaxed and casual way. Mono-syllable verbs are reduplicated in "AA" style, for example 看看, 听听. Double-syllable verbs are reduplicated in "ABAB" style, such as 研究研究 and 学习学习.

3. "如果说中国人的婚礼是红色的，那么是不是可以说，西方人的婚礼是白色的呢？"

"如果说……，那么是不是可以说……"is a selective question composed of two clauses with suppositional relation. But the speaker uses a question because he is not sure if the conclusion of the supposition can be realized.

如果说乘飞机很安全的话，那么是不是可以说，乘火车就更安全了呢？

如果说经常看电脑会伤害眼睛的话，那么是不是可以说，总玩手机更伤害眼睛呢？

Exercise

On your own

1. Match the left and right columns according to the text.

(1) 新娘身上穿着   红色的花儿。

(2) 新娘头上戴着   红色的旗袍。

(3) 墙上挂着   红色的"囍"字。

2. Write the reduplicated form of the following verbs and read aloud.

看、想、听、闻、尝、找、夸、休息、了解、讨论、认识

（闻 = wén = smell）

Conversation practice

1. Can you tell your partner the differences between the two people in the following pictures?

Mack   Tom

Mack 身上穿着黑色的西装……

2. Talk about the wedding with your partner based on the pictures and clues.

(1)   (2) 然后……

朋友A：恭喜、恭喜!   朋友A：祝你们新婚快乐①!

新娘、新郎：欢迎! 欢迎你们。   朋友B：祝你们幸福、快乐②!

---

① I wish you a joyful wedding and a happy marriage!

② I wish you every happiness!

(3) 接下来(jiē xiàlái, next)……

(4) 后来……

朋友A：干杯，为新娘、新郎干杯！

朋友B：干杯，为他们的幸福干杯！

朋友A：新娘的衣服真漂亮！

朋友B：是啊，不过，新娘长得更漂亮。

Class activity & communication task

(1) Find out online the wedding customs in different countries.

(2) Ask your classmates about their experiences of attending weddings. Are the weddings they've been to eastern style or western style?

("你参加的婚礼是中式(eastern style)的还是西式(western style)的？")

(3) Discuss the similarities and differences between eastern and western weddings.

If Chinese wedding is red, then may we say that western wedding is white?

Reading comprehension

1. 杰克夸新娘

杰克：您的新娘长得很漂亮。

新郎：哪里，哪里。

杰克：她的眼睛、鼻子(bízi, nose)都长
得非常漂亮。

新郎：哪里，哪里。

杰克：她的眉毛(méimao, eyebrow)也很
漂亮。

新郎：哪里，哪里。

杰克：她每个地方都很漂亮。

美云：杰克，你让我叔叔很不好意思(bù hǎoyìsi, embarrassed)。

杰克：不可能，他一直在问我"哪里，哪里"。

True or False:

① "哪里，哪里"在这里的意思是"什么地方"。(✓)

② 美云觉得杰克的回答不太合适。(✓)

2. 塞翁失马(The old frontiersman losing his horse)

古时候，有个老人(lǎorén, old man)住在边塞地区(biānsài dìqū, frontier area)。他家有一匹马。有一天，这匹马跑到邻国(línguó, neighbor country)去了，邻居们都来安慰(ānwèi, to comfort)他。他说："这不一定是坏事(huàishì, a bad thing)。"过了几天，这匹马回来了，还带回来一匹好马。邻居都来祝贺(zhùhè, to congratulate)，老人又说："这也不一定是好事(hǎoshì, a good thing)。"

True or False:

① "这不一定是坏事"意思是"这可能是好事。"(✓)

② 最后，塞翁家的马都跑光了。(✗)

Listen and practice

1. Listening comprehension

(1) Decide whether the following statements are true or false after listening to the recording.

Key words:

发现 fāxiàn (to find)

True or false:

① 杰克昨天参加了西方人的婚礼。( )

② 西方的新娘不穿红色的旗袍。(　　)

③ 中国的新娘脚上穿白色的皮鞋。(　　)

④ 中国人结婚的时候门口挂着红色的灯笼。(T)

⑤ 中国人结婚的时候还放鞭炮，这跟西方一样。(F)

(2) Answer the following questions after listening to the recording.

Key words:

酸奶公司 suānnǎi gōngsī (yogurt company)

广告 guǎnggào (advertisement)

又酸又甜 yòu suān yòu tián (both sour and sweet)

初恋 chūliàn (first love)

记者 jìzhě (reporter; journalist)

经理 jīnglǐ (manager)

容易 róngyì (easy)

尝一尝 cháng yi cháng (to have a taste)

Questions:

① 酸奶公司的广告说什么？

② 记者问什么？

③ 经理说什么？

④ 你认为酸奶和"初恋"有什么关系？

2. Read and sing.

掀 起 你 的 盖 头 来
xiān qǐ nǐ de gài tou lái

掀 起 了 你 的 盖 头 来，让 我 看 你 的 眉 毛，
xiān qǐ le nǐ de gài tou lái ràng wǒ kàn nǐ de méi mao

你 的 眉 毛 细 又 长，好 像 树 梢 的 弯 月 亮。
nǐ de méi mao xì yòu cháng hǎo xiàng shù shāo de wān yuè liang

掀 起 了 你 的 盖 头 来，让 我 看 你 的 眼 睛，
xiān qǐ le nǐ de gài tou lái ràng wǒ kàn nǐ de yǎn jing

你 的 眼 睛 明 又 亮，好 像 秋 波 一 般 样。
nǐ de yǎn jing míng yòu liàng hǎo xiàng qiū bō yì bān yàng

掀 起 了 你 的 盖 头 来，让 我 看 你 的 脸 儿，
xiān qǐ le nǐ de gài tou lái ràng wǒ kàn nǐ de liǎn ér

你 的 脸 儿 红 又 圆，好 像 苹 果 到 秋 天。
nǐ de liǎn ér hóng yòu yuán hǎo xiàng píng guǒ dào qiū tiān

Lift up Your Handkerchief

Lift up your handkerchief, and let me see your eyebrows,

They are so fine and neat, just like the crescent moon hanging on the treetop.

Lift up your handkerchief, and let me see your eyes,

They are so clear and bright, just like the autumn ripples.

Lift up your handkerchief, and let me see your cheeks,

They are so rosy and chubby, just like the autumn apples.

掀起你的盖头来

王洛宾词曲

1. 掀 起了你的　盖　头来，　　让　我看你的眉　　毛，
2. 掀 起了你的　盖　头来，　　让　我看你的眼　　睛，
3. 掀 起了你的　盖　头来，　　让　我看你的脸　　儿，

你 的 眉毛　细又长啊，　好 像那树梢的　弯 月 亮，
你 的 眼睛　明又亮啊，　好 像那秋波　一 般 样，
你 的 脸儿　红又圆啊，　好 像那苹果　到 秋 天，

你 的 眉毛　细又长啊，　好 像那树梢的　弯 月 亮。
你 的 眼睛　明又亮啊，　好 像那秋波　一 般 样。
你 的 脸儿　红又圆啊，　好 像那苹果　到 秋 天。

114

Chinese character

Circle the single-element characters in the following chart and write them in the squares.

gōng 恭	yǐ 已	dēng 灯	rú 如	zhuō 桌	hóng 红
lǎo 老	tóng 同	lóng 笼	chuān 穿	xī 西	lǐ 礼
láng 郎	guà 挂	dōng 东	jiù 就	yìng 应	zuó 昨
huā 花	yǒu 友	cháng 长	guǎn 馆	bǎi 摆	hūn 婚
pí 皮	xié 鞋	páo 袍	yuán 员	yí 姨	wèi 为
gāi 该	qiáng 墙	fāng 方	shū 叔	fàng 放	xiǎng 响

巳	西	长	方
为	方		

Firecrackers (*Baozhu* in Chinese)

Setting off firecrackers to celebrate the Spring Festival has a long history tracing back over 2, 000 years ago in China. The earliest firecrackers referred to burning bamboo resulting in explosion. It was so named (*baozhu*—burning bamboo) because burning bamboo created a "pipi papa" sound. Firecrackers also have other names such as *baozhang*, *paozhang* and *bianpao*. It's a long lasting tradition to set off firecrackers to celebrate the Spring Festival. Legend has it that a monster called *nian* appears during the Spring Festival, so people scare the monster away by setting off firecrackers and pasting red couplets.

Firecrackers bring about more happiness and fun to the Spring Festival. Nowadays people set off firecrackers when important ceremonies and celebrations are held in order to add a festive atmosphere. However firecrackers can easily cause environmental pollution and fires. Therefore many restrictive regulations are worked out in many cities although firecrackers are not entirely prohibited.

11 不同的节日，同样的祝贺(zhùhè)

Getting started

Try to figure out the following congratulatory cards and spring couplet.

Happy New Year!

May all your wishes come ture in the next year!

感恩节快乐！

Happy Thanksgiving!

圣诞快乐！

Merry Christmas!

新年快乐！

Happy New Year!

Text 1

Jack and Ma Ming are talking about different festival customs.

杰克：马明，你写汉字写得很好。你能不能帮我写一张贺卡?

马明：当然可以。写什么?

杰克：你帮我想想。我下个星期寄(jì)给在中国的网友。

马明：你有中国网友了? 是女朋友吗?

杰克：别开玩笑(kāi wánxiào)了。因为我收到了网友的圣诞贺卡，我也应该寄出一张春节贺卡。

马明：好吧，不过，我要知道你的网友是一个什么样的人?

杰克：他讲(jiǎng)故事讲得很好，他的性格(xìnggé)可能很开朗(kāilǎng)。

马明：还有呢?

杰克：他知道的事情很多，所以他可能读书读得不少。

马明：我知道了。你等等，我马上就帮你写贺卡。

Text 2

A couplet for the Spring Festival.

春节是中国最重要(zhòngyào)的传统(chuántǒng)节日。每年(měi nián)春节以前的几个星期，人们(rénmen)就开始忙着准备(zhǔnbèi)过节(guòjié)了。孩子们要帮助父母打扫房间，妈妈要准备很多好吃的东西。春节还有一件很重要的事情，就是贴(tiē)春联(chūnlián)。人们把美好(měihǎo)的祝愿(zhùyuàn)写在红色的纸条(zhǐtiáo)上，把纸条贴在门的两边。这就是春联。

例如：

爆竹一声除旧　　春联万户更新
天增岁月人增寿　　春满人间福满门

有人还在门上倒(dào)着贴一个"福(fú)"字，表示"福到了"的意思(yìsi)。

120

New words

1. 祝贺	zhùhè	*v.*	to congratulate
2. 寄	jì	*v.*	to mail; to post
3. 开玩笑	kāi wánxiào		to play/make a joke
4. 讲（故事）	jiǎng (gùshi)	*v.*	to tell (a story)
5. 性格	xìnggé	*n.*	personality
6. 开朗	kāilǎng	*adj.*	sanguine; always cheerful
7. 重要	zhòngyào	*adj.*	important
8. 传统	chuántǒng	*n.*	tradition
9. 每年	měi nián		each year
10. 人们	rénmen	*n.*	people
11. 准备	zhǔnbèi	*v.*	to prepare
12. 过节	guòjié	*v.*	to celebrate a festival
13. 贴	tiē	*v.*	to paste; to stick; to glue
14. 春联	chūnlián	*n.*	couplet for the Spring Festival
15. 美好	měihǎo	*adj.*	beautiful; fine
16. 祝愿	zhùyuàn	*n.*	wish
17. 纸条	zhǐtiáo	*n.*	scroll
18. 倒	dào	*v.*	to reverse; to turn upside down
19. 福	fú	*n.*	blessing; happiness; good luck
20. 意思	yìsi	*n.*	meaning

Notes

1. "天增岁月人增寿，春满人间福满门。"

   This is a couplet given in the text. All couplets must be based on antithesis, a rhetorical device to show two corresponding or similar meanings by using a pair of phrases or sentences with the same number of words, the same structure and symmetrical meaning.

爆竹	一声	除旧
春联	万户	更新

2. "有人还在门上倒着贴一个'福'字，表示'福到了'的意思。"

     It is a unique expression in Chinese language to use a homophone or word with similar pronunciation as a replacement to achieve a better rhetorical effect, given the fact that there exists characters with the same or similar pronunciation. The character 福 is deliberately pasted upside down, and 倒 (upside down) is used to show 到 (arrive).

     A couplet describes poor life as such: the first line reads 二三四五 without 一 in it, and the second line reads 六七八九 without 十 in it. The two lines mean 缺衣少食 (lacking clothes and food), using homophones of 衣 (clothes) to replace 一 (one) and 食 (food) to replace 十 (ten). The horizontal line reads 南北 without 东西 in it. As the two of four direction words, 东西 also has the meaning of THINGS. So the horizontal line means NO MORE THINGS.

Exercise

On your own

Rearrange the following words and phrases according to the texts and then write their numbers in the phoenix's tail to make a complete sentence.

(1) 马明①   写汉字②   很好③   写得④

(2) 杰克①   马明②   帮③   写贺卡④

(3) 杰克的网友① 讲得②   很好③   讲故事④

Conversation practice

The Spring Festival and Christmas

How are the people in the pictures celebrating the Spring Festival and Christmas? What are the similarities and differences? Please discuss them with your partner.

122

Class activity & communication task

1. Activity.

   (1) Work in groups of three to four classmates. Make a PPT on the subject of the Spring Festival or Christmas customs.

   (2) Make a festival card and send it as a gift. Explain what you write on the card.

2. (1) Read aloud and recite.

   上对下，小对大，前后对左右。

   天对地，雨对风，晚照对晴空。

   (2) Divide the students into three groups and then finish the following sentences. The teacher will judge which group is the best one.

   山对_____，云对_____，黄河对_____。

   左对_____，里对_____。高低对_____。

   冷对_____，阴对_____，太阳对_____。

   早对_____，冬对_____，春去对_____。

Reading comprehension

1. 今天是大年初一，杰克一早就到马明家去了。他们家很热闹，来了很多亲戚，大家互相拜年，说了很多祝福的话。马明一家对杰克很好，教他包饺子，马明的爸爸还给了杰克一个红包，说祝他健康快乐。杰克觉得中国人过年真有意思。

(1) 杰克过的是中国的什么节日？（ D ）

    A. 元宵节   B. 端午节   C. 中秋节   D. 春节

(2) 为什么马明的爸爸要给杰克红包？（ C ）

    A. 谢谢杰克的帮助   B. 他们想让马明帮忙买一些东西

    C. 祝福杰克   D. 不知道

2. 一只老虎很饿，它抓住(zhuāzhù, to catch)了一只狐狸(húli, fox)。可是狐狸说："我是上帝的使者(Shàngdì de shǐzhě, God's messenger)，你不能吃我。"老虎不相信，狐狸说："我在前面走，你跟在我后面，你看野兽(yěshòu, wild beast)们怕不怕(pà bu pà, to be afraid or not)我。"老虎同意了。它们走在路上，野兽们看见它们都跑了。老虎相信(xiāngxìn, to believe)了狐狸的话。

(1) 如果用一个成语概括(gàikuò, to summarize)这个故事，应该是：（ C ）

    A. 狐朋狗友(húpéng-gǒuyǒu)   B. 虎虎生威(hǔ hǔ shēng wēi)

    C. 狐假虎威(hújiǎhǔwēi)

(2) 动物都逃跑的原因是：（ A ）

    A. 野兽们害怕老虎   B. 野兽们害怕狐狸

    C. 野兽们害怕狐狸和老虎

Listen and practice

1. Listening comprehension

(1) Decide whether the following statements are true or false after listening to the recording.

True or false:

① 杰克要学汉语，所以他在家门的两边贴春联。(F)

② 杰克请马明帮助他写贺卡。(F)

③ 马明的妈妈请杰克吃东西。(F)

④ 马明写了两副对联，杰克都不喜欢。(F)

(2) Answer the following questions after listening to the recording.

Key words:

小王 Xiǎo Wáng (Xiao Wang)

得到提升 dédào tíshēng (to get a promotion)

好像 hǎoxiàng (as if; to seem; to look like)

忘记 wàngjì (to forget)

年轻人 niánqīng rén (young people)

15年的经验 shíwǔ nián de jīngyàn (15 years of experience)

15次 shíwǔ cì (15 times)

Questions:

① 小王工作了多少年?

② 小王得到提升了吗?

③ 小王为什么很生气?

④ 经理觉得自己做得对吗? 为什么?

2. Read the following ancient poem.

爆 竹 声 中 一 岁 除,
bào zhú shēng zhōng yí suì chú

春 风 送 暖 入 屠 苏。
chūn fēng sòng nuǎn rù tú sū

千 门 万 户 瞳 瞳 日,
qiān mén wàn hù tóng tóng rì

总 把 新 桃 换 旧 符。
zǒng bǎ xīn táo huàn jiù fú

（北宋·王安石《元日》）

> People see off the old year and greet the new year with the sound of firecrackers,
>
> tasty wine adds to the joy brought by the warm spring breeze.
>
> Millions of households greet the rising sun,
>
> and replace the old peach wood charms with the new ones for the new year.

Chinese character

Greet the Spring Festival with a five-happiness red envelope. Find three characters in the dictionary with this same part based on the patterns of the envelope.

（鸟） （马） （𠂉） （贝） （亻）

125

Couplets

Couplets (*Duilian* in Chinese, also called *Duizi*, *Yingtie*, *Yinglian*) are sentences written on scrolls hung, pasted or engraved on the walls, gates or pillars of a hall. Ancient people hung peach wood charms (*Taofu* in Chinese) on the doors to fend off evil, a tradition in which couplets originated. According to the existing information, the earliest couplets appeared during the Five Dynasties (907—960), improved and became popular later and at the same time spread to Japan and Southeast Asia.

As a language art based on Chinese ancient poems, couplets take the form of two vertically written lines, with the right line as the first line and the left line as the second. Couplets have many requirements such as strict antithesis between the first and second lines and the use of homophones in antithesis.

Based on different uses, couplets are divided into the Spring Festival couplets, scenic spots couplets and scholar's study couplets, just to name a few.

12 你更喜欢吃哪一种菜

Getting started

What's your favorite food? What do you usually eat?

两份菜单 Two Menus

(1) Menu of Chinese Dishes

凉菜 liángcài (cold dishes)：

　　熏鱼 xūnyú (smoked fish)

　　拌海带丝 bàn hǎidàisī (kelp salad)

　　白斩鸡 báizhǎnjī (chicken salad)

热菜 rècài (hot dishes) ——素菜 sùcài (vegetables)：

　　蚝油生菜 háoyóu shēngcài (lettuce stir-fried with oyster sauce)

　　炒扁豆 chǎo biǎndòu (stir-fried hyacinth beans)

　　麻婆豆腐 mápó dòufu (pockmarked grandma's tofu)

热菜 rècài (hot dishes) ——荤菜 hūncài (meat)：

　　松鼠桂鱼 sōngshǔ guìyú (squirrel sweet and sour cod)

　　烤鸭 kǎoyā (roast duck)

　　京酱肉丝 jīngjiàng ròusī (shredded pork cooked in soy sauce)

汤 tāng (soup)：

　　鸡蛋汤 jīdàn tāng (egg soup)

　　酸辣汤 suānlà tāng (hot and sour soup)

　　三鲜汤 sānxiān tāng (soup with three delicacies)

主食 zhǔshí (staple food)：

　　米饭 mǐfàn (rice)　　　　　　饺子 jiǎozi (dumplings)

　　包子 bāozi (steamed stuffed bun)　　馒头 mántou (steamed bread)

(2) Menu of Western Dishes

饮料 yǐnliào (soft drink)：

葡萄酒 pútao jiǔ (grape wine)

香蕉丽人 xiāngjiāo lìrén (banana split)

柠檬汁 níngméng zhī (lemonade juice)

汤 tāng (soup)：

奶油汤 nǎiyóu tāng (cream soup)

蘑菇汤 mógu tāng (mushroom soup)

洋葱汤 yángcōng tāng (onion soup)

沙拉 shālā (salad)：

蔬菜沙拉 shūcài shālā (green salad)

水果沙拉 shuǐguǒ shālā (fruit salad)

海鸥沙拉 hǎi'ōu shālā (cobb salad)

热菜 rècài (main course)：

意大利肉酱面 Yìdàlì ròujiàngmiàn (spaghetti)

酥炸鱼柳 sū zhá yúliǔ (crispy fried fish)

炸牛排 zhá niúpái (fried steaks)

甜点 tiándiǎn (desserts)：

水果布丁 shuǐguǒ bùdīng (fruit pudding)

巧克力圣代 qiǎokèlì shèngdài (chocolate sundae)

香草冰激凌 xiāngcǎo bīngjīlíng (vanilla ice cream)

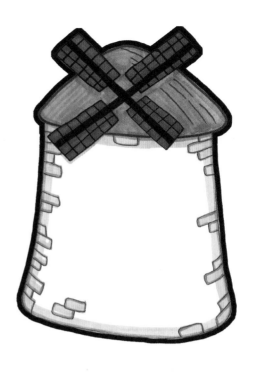

Text 1

Jack and Ma Ming are talking about the different flavors of various dishes.

杰克：马明，我听说，最近流行吃中餐。

马明：对，昨天我刚吃了中国菜。我叔叔请客，他点(diǎn)了六七个菜。

杰克：那么多！

马明：我们先点了一两个凉菜，然后又点了四五个热菜。

杰克：你吃过(guo)日餐吗?

马明：我吃过，日餐和中餐不太一样。

杰克：我喜欢吃墨西哥(Mòxīgē)菜，因为我喜欢吃辣的。

马明：那你也一定喜欢吃中国的川菜(chuāncài)。你吃过法国(Fǎguó)菜吗?

杰克：当然吃过。法国菜我更喜欢。

马明：我听说47街有一家法国饭馆。

杰克：是吗? 你想不想去尝尝法国菜?

马明：我想应该先去挣钱，然后再去吃。

Text 2

Different tableware.

不同的民族有不同的文化。他们的饮食(yǐnshí)习惯不同，使用(shǐyòng)的餐具(cānjù)往往也不同。在中国，人们习惯用筷子(kuàizi)吃饭(chīfàn)。吃饭的时候，一家人坐(zuò)在一起，桌子中间(zhōngjiān)摆着菜，每个人用筷子夹(jiā)菜吃。中国人觉得这样吃饭很热闹。在欧洲(Ōuzhōu)，人们习惯用刀(dāo)、叉(chā)吃饭。每个人吃自己的饭菜。有人说，这样吃饭很卫生(wèishēng)。世界(shìjiè)上还有一些民族，他们不用筷子，也不用刀子和叉子。他们用手抓(zhuā)饭吃。

你用过筷子吗? 你看见过中国人的家庭怎么吃饭吗?

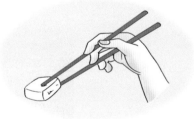

New words

1. 点 (菜)	diǎn (cài)	*v.*	to order (dishes)
2. 过	guo	*pt.*	*used after a verb or an adjective to indicate a past action or state*
3. 饮食	yǐnshí	*n.*	diet
4. 使用	shǐyòng	*v.*	to use
5. 餐具	cānjù	*n.*	tableware
6. 筷子	kuàizi	*n.*	chopstick
7. 吃饭	chīfàn	*v.*	to eat; to have meals
8. 坐	zuò	*v.*	to sit
9. 中间	zhōngjiān	*n.*	middle
10. 夹	jiā	*v.*	to pick up; to press from both sides
11. 刀	dāo	*n.*	knife
12. 叉	chā	*n.*	fork
13. 卫生	wèishēng	*adj.*	good for health; hygienic
14. 世界	shìjiè	*n.*	world
15. 抓	zhuā	*v.*	to take hold with fingers; to clutch

Proper nouns

1. 墨西哥	Mòxīgē	Mexico
2. 川菜	chuāncài	Sichuan Cuisine
3. 法国	Fǎguó	France
4. 欧洲	Ōuzhōu	Europe

1. "他点了六七个菜"。

    六七 in this sentence are two neighboring numbers used to show an approximate number. Words such as 几 and 一些 we've studied before are also approximate numbers, which may take the form of either a one-digit number or a multi-digit number.

    教室里有七八个人。

    这个学校有四五百人。

    这个年级大概有一百三四十人。

    These different numbers show different accuracy.

2. "你吃过日餐吗？"

    Aspect particle 过 can be used after the verb or the adjective, showing certain action happened once or certain state appeared once.

    我去过香港，那儿很热。

    这里曾经热闹过一阵，现在冷清了。

    Its negative form is to add 没 or 没有 before the verb or adjective, showing the action hasn't happened or the state hasn't appeared.

    他没来过这个运动场。

    这里从来没有安静过。

Exercise

On your own

Match the left and right columns according to the text, and then read the sentences.

(1) 马明想先挣钱   习惯用刀叉吃饭。

(2) 中国人   用手抓饭吃。

(3) 欧洲人   然后再去尝法国菜。

(4) 有些民族   习惯用筷子吃饭。

Conversation practice

1. Match the country's name and the pictures. Talk with your partner about the dishes you've tried in various countries.

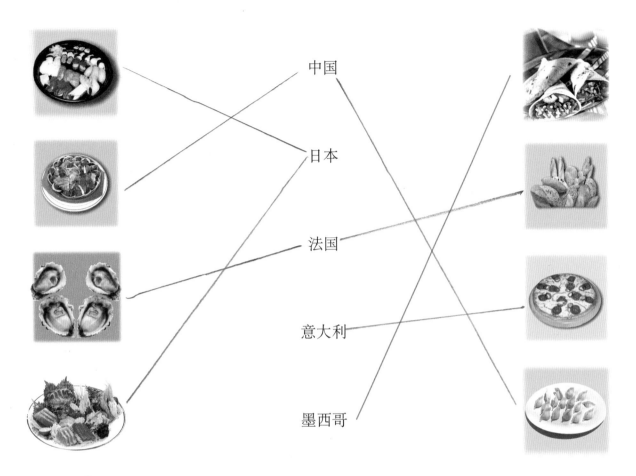

2. Use approximate numbers to answer these questions.

   (1) 你有几个好朋友？

   (2) 有几个亲戚常来你家？

   (3) 咱们学校有多少学生？

Class activity & communication task

   (1) Work in groups of three to four classmates. Find out about the weekly menu of each of their families and fill in the following chart.

   (2) Discuss the differences of the food. One representative shares the discussion result with the class.

	星期一 Monday	星期二 Tuesday	星期三 Wednesday	星期四 Thursday	星期五 Friday	星期六 Saturday	星期天 Sunday
早餐 Breakfast							
午餐 Lunch							
晚餐 Dinner							

Read and talk

饮食习惯

especially　*for example*

　　饮食习惯和文化有关系，在正式的宴会上，各自的特点体现得尤为突出。比如上菜①的顺序就很不相同。中餐会先上凉菜，西餐会先上汤，然后再上其他的菜。当英国人见到茶、中国人见到水果(shuǐguǒ, fruit)时，就知道菜已经上完了。有的美国人习惯把主菜②分为肉类③、海鲜④和蔬菜⑤等，最后用一份甜食⑥作为结束。中餐一般是肉和菜配在一起，做成不同口味的菜。鱼在中餐中是很受欢迎的主菜。

Questions:

(1) 在中国，服务员端上什么的时候，就知道菜已经上完了？

(2) 美国人的主菜分为哪几部分？

(3) 谈一谈你所了解的不同国家餐饮习俗的差异。

---

① 上菜：to serve food

② 主菜：main course

③ 肉类：meat

④ 海鲜：sea food

⑤ 蔬菜：vegetables

⑥ 甜食：sweet food *desert*

Listen and practice

1. Listening comprehension

   (1) Decide whether the following statements are true or false after listening to the recording.

   Key words:

   不同的地方 bùtóng de dìfang (different places/another place)

   差不多 chàbuduō (almost)

   True or False:

   ① 很多民族的饮食习惯差不多。(F)

   ② 中国人吃饭的时候常常吃五六个菜。(F)

   ③ 中国四川的菜和北京的菜差不多。(F)

   ④ 中国人觉得大家一起吃饭很热闹。(T)

   (2) Answer the following questions after listening to the recording.

   Key words:

   山西 Shānxī (Shangxi)   吓一跳 xiàyítiào (shocked)   可怕 kěpà (terrible)

   煮 zhǔ (to boil)   醋 cù (vinegar)   吃醋 chīcù (jealous)

   异性 yìxìng (opposite sex)

   Questions:

   ① "猫耳朵" 是什么？

   ② 珍妮说 "吃醋" 别人为什么会笑?

   ③ 在饭馆需要醋时，应该怎么说?

2. Read the following modern poem.

春 笋， 你 好！
chūn sǔn   nǐ hǎo

在 我 的 记 忆 里，
zài wǒ de jì yì li

年 年 春 天 你 来 得 最 早。
nián nián chūn tiān nǐ lái de zuì zǎo

几 场 春 雨 飘 洒，
jǐ chángchūn yǔ piāo sǎ

春 天 的 竹 林 你 长 得 最 快。
chūn tiān de zhú lín nǐ zhǎng de zuì kuài

在 我 屋 旁 的 竹 林 里，
zài wǒ wū páng de zhú lín li

你 邀 我 一 起 寻 找 绿 色 的 梦。
nǐ yāo wǒ yì qǐ xún zhǎo lǜ sè de mèng

Hello, spring bamboo shoots!
In my memory, you're the one
to come first every spring.
After the spring rains, you're
the one to grow fastest in the
spring woods.
In the woods where my hut is
hiding, you invite me to pur-
sue green dreams.

Chinese character

Guess the riddle.

一口咬掉牛尾巴。(打一字)

Bite off the cow tail in one go. (Guess the character)

Unit Summary

Functional Usage

1. Discussing customs

中 国 人 在 有 喜 事 的 时 候 放 鞭 炮。
zhōng guó rén zài yǒu xǐ shì de shí hou fàng biān pào

2. Customs Comparison

如 果 说 中 国 人 的 婚 礼 是 红 色 的,
rú guǒ shuō zhōng guó rén de hūn lǐ shì hóng sè de

那 么 是 不 是 可 以 说,西 方 人 的 婚
nà me shì bu shì kě yǐ shuō xī fāng rén de hūn

礼 是 白 色 的 呢?
lǐ shì bái sè de ne

在 中 国,人 们 习 惯 用 筷 子 吃 饭。
zài zhōng guó rén men xí guàn yòng kuài zi chī fàn

在 欧 洲,人 们 习 惯 用 刀 叉 吃 饭。
zài ōu zhōu rén men xí guàn yòng dāo chā chī fàn

3. Dissuading

别 开 玩 笑 了。
bié kāi wán xiào le

4. Guessing and estimating

他 的 性 格 可 能 很 开 朗。
tā de xìng gé kě néng hěn kāi lǎng

他 可 能 读 了 很 多 书。
tā kě néng dú le hěn duō shū

GRAMMAR FOCUS

Sentence pattern	*Example*

1. 动词重叠

你 可 以 夸 夸 他 的 新 娘。
nǐ kě yǐ kuā kua tā de xīn niáng

2. 存现句

这 边 挂 着 红 色 的 灯 笼。
zhè biān guà zhe hóng sè de dēng long

3. "如果说……，那么
是不是可以说……"

如 果 说 中 国 人 的 婚 礼 是
rú guǒ shuō zhōng guó rén de hūn lǐ shì

红 色 的，那 么 是 不 是 可 以 说
hóng sè de nà me shì bú shì kě yǐ shuō

西 方 人 的 婚 礼 是 白 色 的 呢?
xī fāng rén de hūn lǐ shì bái sè de ne

4. 谐音词

有 人 还 在 门 上 倒 着 贴 一
yǒu rén hái zài mén shang dào zhe tiē yí

个 "福" 字，表 示 "福 到 了" 的
gè fú zì biǎo shì fú dào le de

意 思。
yì si

5. 对偶表达法

天 增 岁 月 人 增 寿，
tiān zēng suì yuè rén zēng shòu

春 满 人 间 福 满 门。
chūn mǎn rén jiān fú mǎn mén

6. 相邻数字表达概数

他 点 了 六 七 个 菜。
tā diǎn le liù qī gè cài

7. 动态助词 "过"

你 吃 过 日 餐 吗?
nǐ chī guo rì cān ma

CHINESE CHARACTERS REVIEW

汉字 Chinese Character		拼音 *Pinyin*	词语组合 Language Composition	
笼	竹 龙	lóng	灯笼	笼子
鞭	革 便	biān	鞭子	鞭炮
响	口 向	xiǎng	音响	响动
恭	共 小	gōng	恭敬	恭喜
夸	大 亏	kuā	夸奖	夸赞
新	亲 斤	xīn	新鲜	新娘
花	艹 化	huā	鲜花	花钱
墙	士 啬	qiáng	墙上	墙壁
摆	扌 罢	bǎi	摆放	摆动
礼	礻 乚	lǐ	婚礼	礼貌
姨	女 夷	yí	阿姨	姨妈
传	亻 专	chuán	传统	传说
贴	贝 占	tiē	贴住	粘贴
贺	加 贝	hè	贺卡	祝贺
洲	氵 州	zhōu	欧洲	大洲

Unit Five

Diet and Health

13 我把菜谱(càipǔ)带来了

Getting started

Read the following recipe and then tell how to cook this dish.

一份菜谱 (A Recipe)

原料： 豆腐 300 克、肉 50 克
作料： 红辣椒 4 个、花生油 20 克、盐 8 克、
　　　水淀粉 5 克、酱油 10 克、花椒粉 2 克、
　　　大蒜 3 瓣

做法：

(1) 把豆腐切成方块

(2) 把肉、蒜、辣椒切碎

(3) 把锅放在火上，放油

(4) 油热以后，炒肉，然后放辣椒、蒜

(5) 放豆腐煮 2 分钟，放水淀粉，花椒粉

Ingredients:　tofu 300 g、beef 50 g

Condiments: red chilli peppers 4，peanut oil 20 g，salt 8 g，water starch 5 g，

　　　　　　soy sauce 10 g，Chinese prickly powder 2 g，garlic 3 pieces

Methods:

(1) Dice the tofu.

(2) Chop the beef, the garlic and the peppers into small pieces.

(3) Put a wok on the heat and then pour in the oil.

(4) After the oil is heated up, stir-fry the beef and then add the pepper and garlic.

(5) Boil the tofu for 2 minutes and then put in the water starch and the Chinese
　　prickly powder.

Text 1

Ma Ming and Meiyun come to Jack's home. They are going to cook Chinese food together.

马明： 时间不早了，我们该吃饭了。

杰克： 我们自己做吧。你们说过要教(jiāo)我做中国菜，是不是忘了？

马明： 没忘。我应该先学会了，再教你。可是我还没学会呢！

美云： 没关系(méi guānxi)，我们一起学。你们看，我把菜谱带来了。

马明： 那太好了。我们选一个简单(jiǎndān)的菜吧。

美云： 麻婆豆腐(mápó dòufu)怎么样？

杰克： 好，现在我们听你的。

美云： 马明，你来切(qiē)豆腐，把豆腐切成方块(fāngkuài)。杰克，你把锅(guō)拿来，别忘了拿作料(zuòliao)来。

Text 2

Can you cook Chinese food?

　　你会做中国菜吗？如果你想学习做中国菜，你应该先找到一个菜谱，然后把需要的原料(yuánliào)买来，再把它们(tāmen)洗干净以后，按照(ànzhào)菜谱把原料切好，准备好作料再开始做。中国菜重视(zhòngshì)色、香、味(sè，xiāng，wèi)。例如"鱼香肉丝"(yúxiāng ròusī)，有漂亮的红色和黄色，鱼(yú)一样的香味(xiāngwèi)和又酸(suān)又辣(là)的味道(wèidào)。你想不想尝尝？

New words

1. 菜谱	càipǔ	*n.*	recipe
2. 教	·jiāo	*v.*	to teach
3. 没关系	méi guānxi		it doesn't matter
4. 简单	jiǎndān	*adj.*	simple
5. 切	·qiē	*v.*	to cut; to chop
6. 方块	fāngkuài	*n.*	square piece
7. 锅	guō	*n.*	pot; wok
8. 作料	zuòliao	*n.*	condiments; seasonings
9. 原料	yuánliào	*n.*	raw material; ingredient
10. 它们	tāmen	*pron.*	they; them (referring to things or animals)
11. 按照	ànzhào	*prep.*	according to
12. 重视	·zhòngshì	*v.*	to attach importance to; to pay attention to
13. 色、香、味	sè, xiāng, wèi		color, smell and flavor
14. 鱼	yú	*n.*	fish
15. 香味	xiāngwèi	*n.*	delicious / fragrant scent
16. 酸	suān	*adj.*	sour
17. 辣	là	*adj.*	chilli; hot
18. 味道	wèidào	*n.*	flavor; taste

Proper nouns

1. 麻婆豆腐	mápó dòufu	pockmarked grandma's tofu
2. 鱼香肉丝	yúxiāng ròusī	fish-flavored shredded pork

1. "我把菜谱带来了。"

    We studied the 把 sentence in Book Two. This is also a 把 sentence, with the only difference of an extra directional complement 来 after the verb 带 .

    你把这本书拿去吧。

    他把老师请进来了。

2. "你应该先找到一个菜谱，然后把需要的原料买来，再把它们洗干净……"

    The "先……然后……再……" structure in this sentence is generally used to show the sequence of the actions. The structure is often used in sentences of describing certain process.

    你可以先去商店看看，然后上网查一查，最后再决定买不买。

    我打算先参加考试，然后去旅行，再回国找工作。

Exercise

On your own

1. Match the left and right columns according to the text.

    (1) 美云、马明和杰克   然后再教杰克。

    (2) 鱼香肉丝   又酸又辣。

    (3) 马明想自己先学会   打算做麻婆豆腐。

2. Picture description
   Use "先……然后……再……" and "把" sentence to explain the process of cooking fricd tomato with eggs.

1.   2.

3.

4.

5.

Conversation practice

Practice with your partner. Complete the conversation, and practice reminding others.

(1) A：现在晚上十二点了，*it's 12 at night now,* ni ba feiji piao 打印 *dayin* chu lai ba。✓

B：(hao de) wo dou da yin wan 了。✓。

(2) A：你别忘了明天要 ~~起~~ zao chi, ba suoyou de xin dou ji chu qu. ✓

B：hao de, na wo guo yi hu'er jiu shui jiao。✓

(3) A：Ni bie wan le Jie Maming，我们今天要一起看电影。

B：wo dou ba ta de dizhi ji xia lai le。

Class activity & communication task

(1) Organize a luncheon party in class. Each student will bring a dish that he/she cooked to class and share it with other classmates.

(2) One representative from each group shares with the class how the dish is prepared. (Prepare some pictures of your cooking process or video)

(3) Vote for the best dish and the best cooking introduction. Make comments.

Read and talk

中国胃 (wèi，stomach)

对于很多华人来说，尽管在西方住了很长时间，"西化"程度很深，但他们仍然有个"中国胃"。据说，上世纪80年代许多中国年轻人刚来到西方留学时很兴奋，因为当时在国内比较少见的麦当劳、肯德基、汉堡王等西式快餐店在这里到处都是，但时间一长他们就吃腻(nì, to be bored)了。《环球时报》曾经报道过，一个中国留学生刚来英国时，兴奋地对记者说："伦敦这儿真好，麦当劳不用排队，'巨无霸'(jùwúbà, Big Mac)和中餐馆炒菜(chǎocài, stir-fry, a fried dish)一个价，这回我可以吃个够了。"可没出两个月，他就开始抱怨："吃伤(shāng, bored)了，吃伤了，回国再也不吃了。"

Questions:

① "很多华人依然有一个'中国胃'"的意思是什么？

② "吃伤了"的意思是什么？

③ 你是什么"胃"？

Listen and practice

1. Listening comprehension

   (1) Decide whether the following statements are true or false after listening to the recording.

   Key words:

   中国菜 Zhōngguó cài (Chinese food)

   洗豆腐 xǐ dòufu (to wash the tofu)

   做一次试试 zuò yí cì shìshi (to have a try)

   True or false:

   ① 杰克和美云来到马明家，他们要学习做中国菜。(**F**)

   ② 他们要学习做麻婆豆腐。(**F**)

   ③ 马明拿来了锅和豆腐。(   )

   ④ 麻婆豆腐的颜色是黄色和白色。(   )

   ⑤ 麻婆豆腐的味道不太辣。(   )

   (2) Answer the following questions after listening to the recording.

   Key words:

   晚饭 wǎnfàn (dinner)

147

洗碗 xǐ wǎn (to wash dishes)

看电视 kàn diànshì (to watch TV)

盘子摔碎 pānzi shuāisuì (the plate dropped and was broken)

姐姐 jiějie (elder sister)

Questions:

① 妈妈和美云在哪里?

② 爸爸和美华在哪里?

③ 厨房里有什么声音?

④ 美华为什么说是妈妈摔碎了盘子?

2. Read the following ancient poem.

渭 城 朝 雨 浥 轻 尘，
wèi chéng zhāo yǔ yì qīng chén

客 舍 青 青 柳 色 新。
kè shè qīng qīng liǔ sè xīn

劝 君 更 尽 一 杯 酒，
quàn jūn gèng jìn yì bēi jiǔ

西 出 阳 关 无 故 人。
xī chū yáng guān wú gù rén

（唐·王维《送元二使安西》）

Dusts are washed off in town by morning rain; The inn is all green where fresh willows reign.

Would you please have more wine, another glass? You'll find no more old friends west of the Pass.

Chinese characters

Look at the food and write Chinese characters. Try your best to write the corresponding characters related to the following pictures about Chinese food.

Cuisines in China

China enjoys a long history of food culture. In this vast country, different regions present different eating habits and customs. In the early years of the Spring and Autumn Period and the Warring States Period, food culture of the Han people already showed differences between the northern and southern styles, which evolved into the northern system and the southern system at the Tang and Song Dynasties. Given the influence of geographical environment, climate and farm produces, and cultural traditions, food of a particular region has, over the years, formed a local feature with great similarity in dishes and a high popularity among people, and this is what cuisine means.

The "eight major cuisines" are the most well-known ones in China include Shandong, Sichuan, Cantonese, Fujian, Jiangsu, Zhejiang, Hunan and Anhui cuisines. They all have different features. To name Sichuan cuisine as an example, it is known for hot and spicy taste as well as for emphasizing color, fragrance, flavor and shape. And "flavor" is given particular attention by combining a numb tongue feeling, and spicy, salty, sweet, sour, bitter, and fragrant tastes.

14 一次体检(tǐjiǎn)

Getting started

How is the health of the person indicated in the physical examination form?

姓　名 xìng míng	性　别 xìng bié	年　龄 nián líng	职　业 zhí yè	住　址 zhù zhǐ
马　照　明 mǎ zhào míng	男 nán	48	工　程　师 gōng chéng shī	春　田　市 81 街　2351号 chūn tián shì　jiē　hào
心　脏 xīn zàng	肺　部 fèi bù	血　液 xuè yè	大　便 dà biàn	小　便 xiǎo biàn
心　电　图 xīn diàn tú 不　正　常 bú zhèng cháng	X　光 guāng 照　片 zhào piàn			

Name	Gender	Age	Occupation	Address
Ma Zhaoming	Male	Forty eight	engineer	No. 2351, 81st street, Springfield City
Heart	**Lung**	**Blood**	**Stool**	**Urine**
Electrocardiogram Abnormal	X-ray film			

Text 1

Ma Ming's parents dispute.

马太太： 你今天见到张医生了吗？

马先生： 见到了。他给我检查了身体，还化验(huàyàn)了血(xiě)。

马太太： 结果(jiéguǒ)怎么样？

马先生： 问题不大。血的化验结果还没看到，这是心脏(xīnzàng)和肺(fèi)的检查结果。

马太太： 谁说问题不大？你的心脏以前就不好，现在肺也有问题了。

马先生： 别大惊小怪(dàjīng-xiǎoguài)的，这点儿小问题没什么。

马太太： 这不是小问题。你应该戒(jiè)烟(yān)，也别再喝酒(jiǔ)了。

马先生： 没那么严重(yánzhòng)吧。

马太太： 等到严重就晚了。

Text 2

Ma Ming is telling his friends about one of his father's physical examinations.

我爸爸昨天到医院(yīyuàn)做了一次体检。他以前心脏不太好，现在肺也有点儿问题了。医生让他戒烟，还建议他经常锻炼身体，去郊外(jiāowài)呼吸(hūxī)新鲜(xīnxiān)空气(kōngqì)。可是他总是觉得自己的健康没有那么糟糕，他认为(rènwéi)医生说得太严重了。他回到家，把这个情况告诉了妈妈。妈妈很吃惊(chījīng)，看到爸爸的态度，她也很生气。

1. 体检	tǐjiǎn	*n.*	physical examination
2. 化验	huàyàn	*v.*	to test; to examine
3. 血	xiě	*n.*	blood
4. 结果	jiéguǒ	*n.*	result
5. 心脏	xīnzàng	*n.*	heart
6. 肺	fèi	*n.*	lung
7. 大惊小怪	dàjīng-xiǎoguài		to be surprised or alarmed at sth. quite normal; to make a fuss about nothing
8. 戒	jiè	*v.*	to give up; to drop; to stop
9. 烟	yān	*n.*	cigarette; pipe tobacco or smoke
10. 酒	jiǔ	*n.*	alcoholic drink
11. 严重	yánzhòng	*adj.*	serious
12. 医院	yīyuàn	*n.*	hospital
13. 郊外	jiāowài	*n.*	suburbs; outskirts
14. 呼吸	hūxī	*v.*	to breathe
15. 新鲜	xīnxiān	*adj.*	fresh
16. 空气	kōngqì	*n.*	air
17. 认为	rènwéi	*v.*	to think
18. 吃惊	chījīng	*v.*	to be startled; to be shocked; to be amazed

Notes

1. "谁说问题不大？"

Interrogative pronoun 谁 in this sentence means anybody, so it can refer to anyone.

谁也不知道他到哪儿去了。

不论谁都得遵守纪律。

我谁也没看见。（我没看见任何人）

2. "谁说问题不大？"

This is a rhetorical question, which shows an affirmative meaning using a question. Moreover, a rhetorical question has a stronger tone than a general declarative sentence, and its answer is the only affirmative one which needn't be answered.

老师难道不应该严格要求自己吗?

这么远的路，我怎么能走得到呢?

3. "这点儿小问题没什么。"

It is mentioned before that the pronoun 什么 can mean anything. For example，什么人都没来 means nobody comes. 没什么 means no problem, it doesn't matter or no big deal.

他觉得上不上大学没什么。

跑步很累，不过累点儿也没什么。

Exercise

On your own

1. Rearrange the following words and phrases according to the texts and then write their numbers in the phoenix's tail to make a complete sentence.

(1) 已经①　　看到了②　　马先生③　　检查结果④

(2) 马太太①　　问题②　　觉得③　　很严重④

(3) 马先生①　　觉得②　　大惊小怪③　　马太太④

2. Picture description

Dad would not listen to any advice...

Conversation practice

Complete the sentence. Express an attitude of disapproval.

(1) A：他怎么还没到啊，真让人着急。

   B：_____。

(2) A：明天要考试了，你还不去学习？

   B：_____。

(3) A：我太担心他的病了。

   B：_____

Class activity & communication task

(1) Work in groups of three to four classmates. Discuss which lifestyle helps people to keep fit based on the clues given.

姓名 _____ 身高 _____(米) 体重_____(千克)			
最近体检时的健康情况： 非常好 □ 比较好 □ 一般 □ 有一点儿问题 □ 问题很严重 □			
	经常	有时候	很少
生活习惯： 锻炼身体吗?	□	□	□
早睡早起吗?	□	□	□
吃蔬菜吗?	□	□	□
喝可乐吗?	□	□	□
喜欢生气吗?	□	□	□
心情愉快吗?	□	□	□

(2) Write a play about the situation where people argue over the same lifestyle which some people deem important while others disagree. Share your performance with the class.

(3) Retell the performance.

Reading comprehension

爸爸：这是我的体检结果，你看看，没什么大问题。

妈妈：谁说问题不大？你应该戒烟、戒酒，每天锻炼身体。

"谁说问题不大"这句话的意思是（ C ）

A. 妈妈想知道"问题不大"这句话是谁说的。

B. 妈妈认为爸爸的身体没问题。

C. 妈妈认为爸爸的身体有问题。

D. 爸爸觉得自己的身体没问题。

Read and perform

Work in groups of three classmates. Read the following story about an idiom. Adapt the story into a drama. The conversations should give expression to the argument between the seller and the audience.

自相矛盾 (zìxiāng-máodùn，Contradict oneself)

古时候有个人，他卖矛 (máo，spear)，也卖盾 (dùn，shield)。别人来买矛的时候，他就夸自己的矛。他说："我的矛可以刺穿 (cìchuān，to stab through) 所有 (suǒyǒu，all) 的盾。"顾客来买盾的时候，他又夸自己的盾。他说："所有的矛都不能刺穿我的盾。"这时候，有一个人问他："如果用你的矛刺你的盾呢？"这个人回答不出来了。

Listen and practice

1. Listening comprehension

(1) Decide whether the following statements are true or false after listening to the recording.

Key words:

请问您是哪一位 qǐngwèn nín shì nǎ yí wèi (Who are you)

丈夫 zhàngfu (husband)

心脏病 xīnzàngbìng (heart disease)

跟他谈 gēn tā tán (to talk with him)

True or false:

① 这是马医生和张太太的谈话。(F)

② 马先生的身体不太好。(T)

③ 马先生吸烟，他也喝酒。(F)

④ 马先生认为自己的身体很糟糕。(F)

⑤ 医生建议马先生经常锻炼身体。(T)

(2) Answer the following questions after listening to the recording.

Key words:

收音机 shōuyīnjī (radio)	温柔 wēnróu (gentle)	肤色 fūsè (complexion)
绒毛 róngmáo (down)	细嫩 xìnèn (delicate)	柔软 róuruǎn (soft)
镜子 jìngzi (mirror)	播音员 bōyīnyuán (announcer)	讲座 jiǎngzuò (lecture)

Questions:

① 小明写完作业后做什么?

② 播音员说什么状况是健康的?

③ 小明觉得自己健康吗?

④ 播音员讲的是关于什么的健康?

2. Read and sing.

阿 里 山 的 姑 娘①
ā　lǐ　shān　de　gū　niang

高 山 青，涧 水 蓝，
gāo shān qīng jiàn shuǐ lán

阿 里 山 的 姑 娘 美 如 水，
ā　lǐ　shān　de　gū　niang měi　rú　shuǐ

阿 里 山 的 少 年② 壮 如 山。
ā　lǐ　shān　de　shào nián zhuàng rú　shān

阿 里 山 的 姑 娘 美 如 水，
ā　lǐ　shān　de　gū　niang měi　rú　shuǐ

阿 里 山 的 少 年 壮 如 山。
ā　lǐ　shān　de　shào niánzhuàng rú　shān

高 山 长 青，涧 水 长 蓝，
gāo shānchángqīng jiàn shuǐ cháng lán

姑 娘 和 那 少 年 永 不 分，
gū　niang hé　nà　shào nián yǒng bù　fēn

碧 水 长 围 着 青 山 转。
bì　shuǐ cháng wéi zhe qīng shānzhuàn

Lasses of Mount Ali

Green mountains, blue waters.

The lasses of Mount Ali are as beautiful as the waters.

The lads of Mount Ali are as strong as the mountains.

The lasses of Mount Ali are as beautiful as the waters.

The lads of Mount Ali are as strong as the mountains.

The mountains will always be green and the waters blue.

The lass and the lad will never be apart.

Just like the blue water is always flowing around the green mountain.

---

① The word 姑娘 is more informal than 女孩子，it may be translated as "Lass".

② The word 少年 is more informal than 男孩子，it may be translated as "Lad".

阿里山的姑娘

佚 名词曲

159

碧水 长 围着青 山 转。哪

嘿! 哈伊那拉哈伊呀 伊呀那伊哟 呀

嗬, 那 伊瓦到依鲁那呀

好 伊呀嗨, 那鲁 娃 哎罗伊拉那呀 嗬嗨呀, 嗬伊那鲁

娃 伊都嗨呀那呀嗬 嗨呀! 高 山 长

青 涧水长 蓝,

姑娘和那少 年 永不分呀, 碧水长 围着

1.
青 山 转。 嘿!

2.
转。

Chinese character

Replace one part of the following characters to turn them into other characters.

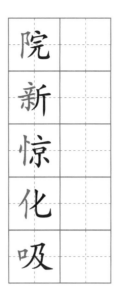

肺	腿
检	
健	
结	
烟	

院	
新	
惊	
化	
吸	

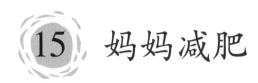 **妈妈减肥**

Getting started

What is your opinion of weightloss and dieting? How does one keep himself/herself fit?

Text 1

Food and diet.

李太太：美云，美华，吃饭了。

美　华：妈妈，今天晚饭我们吃什么？

李太太：红烧肉 (hóngshāoròu)、宫保鸡丁 (gōngbǎo jīdīng)，还有一条
　　　　大鲤鱼 (lǐyú)。

美　云：又是红烧肉！太腻 (nì) 了。再这样吃，我也会变成
　　　　(biànchéng) 胖子 (pàngzi) 的。

李太太：一点儿也不腻。吃红烧肉还可以美容 (měiróng) 呢。

美　云：我不爱吃红烧肉，你们吃吧。

李太太：大家都说我这几天又胖了，该减肥了，我也不吃了。

李先生：昨天你就说不再吃肉了，可是今天又烧了这么多肉，这
　　　　不是自相矛盾 (zìxiāng-máodùn) 吗？

Text 2

Acting in a way that defeats one's purpose — Meiyun is telling a story about her mother trying to lose weight.

今天妈妈又从卧室拿出好几件衣服。我知道，她又长胖了，这几件衣服已经不能穿了。她常常说："我该减肥了。"她也常常看减肥广告，了解新的减肥方法(fāngfǎ)。可是每次上街(shàngjiē)，她都买回来许多好吃的东西，比如巧克力 (qiǎokèlì)、奶油(nǎiyóu)蛋糕什么的。每天做饭，她都做许多好吃的，包括她最有名(yǒumíng)的菜——红烧肉。我爸爸说她这是"南辕北辙(nányuán-běizhé)"。

最近我妈妈正在了解怎样(zěnyàng)用中药(zhōngyào)减肥呢！她说这样减肥最安全，也比较方便。

164

New words

1. 鲤鱼	lǐyú	*n.*	carp
2. 腻	nì	*adj.*	oily; greasy
3. 变成	biànchéng	*v.*	to become
4. 胖子	pàngzi	*n.*	overweight person
5. 美容	měiróng	*v.*	to improve one's looks
6. 自相矛盾	zìxiāng-máodùn		to contradict oneself
7. 方法	fāngfǎ	*n.*	method
8. 上街	shàngjiē	*v.*	to go shopping
9. 巧克力	qiǎokèlì	*n.*	chocolate
10. 奶油	nǎiyóu	*n.*	cream
11. 有名	yǒumíng	*adj.*	well-known; famous
12. 南辕北辙	nányuán-běizhé		to try to go south by driving north; to act in a way that defeats one's purpose
13. 怎样	zěnyàng	*pron.*	how
14. 中药	zhōngyào	*n.*	Chinese medicine

Proper nouns

1. 红烧肉	hóngshāoròu	*n.*	pork braised in brown sauce
2. 宫保鸡丁	gōngbǎo jīdīng	*n.*	spicy diced chicken with peanuts; kung pao chicken

Notes

1. "又是红烧肉！"

   The adverb 又, put before the verb, can show different meanings. In this sentence, 又 shows the repetition of the situation. On the other hand, it also shows a feeling that the speaker is not very satisfied with 吃红烧肉.

   他又来了。

   你怎么又打开电视了？

165

2. "一点儿也不腻。"

"'一点儿不' + Adjective" shows a very low degree. The structure is a complete negation.

这个公园一点儿也不漂亮。

说是打折，其实东西一点儿也不便宜。

这个菜一点儿也不好吃。

3. "吃红烧肉还可以美容呢。"

Auxiliary verb 可以 in this sentence shows a certain use.

木材可以造纸。

电脑可以用来玩游戏。

吃鱼可以降血脂。

不能 is often used in negation.

吃鱼不能降血脂。

4. "吃红烧肉还可以美容呢。"

The modal particle 呢 is used at the end of this sentence to indicate fact, often with exaggeration.

我还没吃饭呢。

那个建筑有三百多米高呢。

Exercise

On your own

1. Use 又 to complete the sentences.

   (1) 他刚喝了咖啡，现在 _又 shuì bù jǎo le,_____。

   (2) 他昨天吃了蛋糕，今天 _又 吃_____。

   (3) 她上个星期买了衣服，这个星期_____。

2. Complete the sentence using 一点儿也不.

   (1) 妈妈很喜欢吃红烧肉，她觉得_____。(腻)

   (2) 他每天都喝咖啡，他觉得_____。(苦)

   (3) 他喜欢爬山，觉得_____。(累)

166

Conversation practice

1. Do you think it's good to lose weight? What do you think of losing weight? Communicate with
   your partner.

减肥好，瘦了以后更漂亮。

减肥好，买衣服更容易。

减肥对身体不好，吃减肥药不安全。

减肥不好，要花很多钱和时间。

2. Stage a performance based on the pictures.

Mum's Diet Plans

①

唉！我又长胖了，我该减肥了！

(Try to act in front of a mirror, stroke your face, hold your waist, then shake your head and say...)

②

这种药不错，用中药减肥，对身体没有副作用。

(When eating chocolates, pay attention to the gradual change: first firmly decide to eat one piece only, then hesitate due to the temptation, finally eat a lot and decide to lose weight later.)

Class activity & communication task

食 谱

肉类： 猪 肉　　牛 肉　　鸡 肉　　鱼 虾
zhū ròu　niú ròu　jī ròu　yú xiā
meat　　beef　　chicken　fish & shirmp

主食： 米 饭　　面 包　　蛋 糕　　玉 米　　薯 条
mǐ fàn　miàn bāo　dàn gāo　yù mǐ　shǔ tiáo
rice　　bread　　cake　　corn　French fries

麦 片
mài piàn
oatmeal

水果： 西 瓜　　梨　　葡 萄　　桃　　苹 果　　香 蕉
xī guā　lí　pú tao　táo　píng guǒ　xiāng jiāo
watermelon peach　grapes　pear　apple　banana

甜食： 巧 克 力　　糖　　口 香 糖　　糕 点　　布 丁
qiǎo kè lì　táng　kǒu xiāng táng　gāo diǎn　bù dīng
chocolate　candy　chewing gum　cakes　pudding

蔬菜： 黄 瓜　　冬 瓜　　茄 子　　萝 卜　　西 红 柿
huáng guā　dōng guā　qié zi　luó bo　xī hóng shì
cucumber　melon　eggplant　radish　tomato

芹 菜　　胡 萝 卜　　白 菜　　芦 笋　　辣 椒
qín cài　hú luó bo　bái cài　lú sǔn　là jiāo
celery　carrot　cabbage　asparagus　pepper

饮料： 牛 奶　　咖 啡　　可 乐　　绿 茶　　豆 浆
niú nǎi　kā fēi　kě lè　lù chá　dòu jiāng
milk　coffee　cola　green tea　soya bean milk

果 汁　　矿 泉 水
guǒ zhī　kuàng quán shuǐ
juice　mineral water

(1) Divide the class into three to four groups. Work out healthy and unhealthy menus.

(2) Present your menus to the class. Introduce your group's views on healthy food.

(3) Compare other groups' introduction. Discuss the similarities and differences between their points.

Reading comprehension

　　我不喜欢吃巧克力，因为太甜了，吃多了会腻。可是妈妈很喜欢巧克力，每天都吃很多，她觉得巧克力一点儿也不腻。因为吃得太多，妈妈越来越胖了，我们很担心她的健康。

True or False:

① 虽然巧克力很甜，但是"我"还是很喜欢。(　　)

② 妈妈吃了太多巧克力，所以健康会受到影响。(　　)

Read and perform

半途而废

(bàntú'érfèi，Give up halfway. / Leave something unfinished.)

　　古时候有个人叫乐羊子，他到很远的地方去学习。学习生活很辛苦(xīnkǔ, hardworking)，他没有学完就回家了。他的妻子正在织布(zhībù, to weave cloth)，听说他没有学完，就把织布机(zhībùjī, loom)上的布剪断(jiǎnduàn, to snip)了。妻子说，学习半途而废，就好像剪断的布，白白浪费(làngfèi, to waste)了很多时间。听了妻子的话，乐羊子马上离开家，继续学习去了。

True or False:

① 乐羊子学习很累，生活条件不好。(　　)

② 乐羊子的妻子常常生气，一生气就把布剪断了。(　　)

③ 乐羊子很害怕妻子，所以赶快离开家走了。(　　)

Listen and practice

1. Listening comprehension

　(1) Decide whether the following statements are true or false after listening to the recording.

　　Key words:

　　饭馆 fànguǎn (restaurant)

　　心情好 xīnqíng hǎo (in a good mood)

　　心宽体胖 xīnkuān-tǐpán (fit and happy)

　　广告 guǎnggào (advertisement)

True or False:

① 饭馆做的红烧鲤鱼比我太太做的好吃。（ F ）

② 因为她喜欢吃，所以她很胖。（ T ）

③ 我太太每次上街都买回来很多衣服。（ F ）

④我喜欢吃肉，也喜欢吃糖。（ F ）

⑤ 我太太常常了解减肥的方法。（ T ）

(2) Answer the following questions after listening to the recording.

Key words:

顾客 gùkè (customer)

新建的大楼 xīn jiàn de dà lóu (a new building)

座 zuò (a measure word for mountains, buildings etc.)　　　　层 céng (storey)

价钱 jiàqián (price)　　　　管理员 guǎnlǐyuán (a manager)

满意 mǎnyì (satisfied)　　　　第五层 dì-wǔ céng (the fifth floor)

Questions:

① 这座大楼一共有几层?

② 每一层的价钱是多少?

③ 顾客对这座大楼满意吗?

④ 顾客为什么想住在第五层?

2. Read and sing

达 坂 城 的 姑 娘
dá　bǎn chéng　de　　gū niang

达	坂	城	的	石	路	平	又	平	啊，	西	瓜	大	又	甜	啊。
dá	bǎn	chéng	de	shí	lù	píng	yòu	píng	a	xī	guā	dà	yòu	tián	a
那	里	出	的	姑	娘	辫	子	长	啊，	两	个	眼	睛	真	漂	亮。
nà	lǐ	chū	de	gū	niang	biàn	zi	cháng	a	liǎng	ge	yǎn	jing	zhēn	piào	liang
你	要	是	嫁	人	不	要	嫁	给	别	人，	一	定	要	嫁	给	我，
nǐ	yào	shi	jià	rén	bù	yào	jià	gěi	bié	rén	yí	dìng	yào	jià	gěi	wǒ
带	着	你	的	钱	财，	领	着	你	的	妹	妹，	赶	上	那	马	车	来。
dài	zhe	nǐ	de	qián	cái	lǐng	zhe	nǐ	de	mèi	mei	gǎn	shàng	nà	mǎ	chē	lái

达坂城的姑娘

王洛宾词曲

达坂城的石路 平又平啊，西瓜大又 甜 啊。

那里出的姑 娘 辫子长 啊，两个眼睛真漂 亮。

你 要是嫁人 不要嫁给别人，一定要 嫁给 我，

带着你的钱 财，领着你的妹 妹，赶上那马 车 来。

Chinese characters

Make the characters slimmer. Cut one part of the following characters to turn them into other characters.

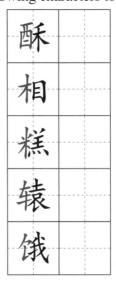

烧	火
鲤	
油	
样	
腻	

酥	
相	
糕	
辕	
饿	

Daban's Girls

Daban's roads are flat and flat, its watermelons are sweet.

Daban's girls have long hairs, their eyes are really pretty.

If you marry don't marry another, be sure to marry me.

Bring your wealth, bring your younger sister, come by horse and carriage.

Chinese culture

Food Therapy

Food is closely related to people's health. In China, the Traditional Chinese Medicine has always emphasized the relationship between a rational diet and good health. Meanwhile, TCM pays great attention to using food with medicinal value or adding certain medicine into diet to get rid of sickness and improve body health. This is what we call "*yaoshan* (medicinal food)" or "*shiliao* (food therapy)". Many food ingredients can be used in "medicinal food" in daily life. For example, radish helps digestion, ginger can fend off coldness and cure cold, and date can invigorate energy, nourish the blood and tranquilize the mind. These experience, accumulated over the past thousands of years, are part of TCM as well as Chinese food culture.

UNIT SUMMARY

FUNCTIONAL USAGE

1. Reminding

别 忘 了 拿 作 料 来。
bié wàng le　ná　zuò liao lái

再 这 样 吃，我 也 会 变 成 胖 子 的。
zài zhè yàng chī　wǒ　yě　huì biàn chéng pàng zi　de

2. Processing

你 应 该 先 找 到 一 个 菜 谱，然 后 把 需 要 的 原
nǐ　yīng gāi xiān zhǎo dào　yí　gè　cài pǔ　　rán hòu　bǎ　xū yào de yuán

料 买 来，再 把 它 们 洗 干 净。
liào mǎi lái　zài　bǎ　tā men　xǐ　gān jìng

3. Showing disapproval

别 大 惊 小 怪 的，这 点 儿 小 问 题 没 什 么。
bié　dà　jīng xiǎo guài de　zhè diǎnr　xiǎo wèn　tí　méi shén me

没 那 么 严 重 吧。
méi　nà　me　yán zhòng ba

4. Arguing

问题不大。——谁说问题不大？
wèn tí bú dà　　shéi shuō wèn tí bú dà

这点儿小问题没什么。——这不是小问题！
zhè diǎnr xiǎo wèn tí méi shén me　　zhè bú shì xiǎo wèn tí

没那么严重吧。——等到严重就晚了！
méi nà me yán zhòng ba　　děng dào yán zhòng jiù wǎn le

5. Expressing difference in opinion

又吃红烧肉，太腻了。
yòu chī hóng shāo ròu　tài nì le

一点儿也不腻。
yì diǎnr yě bú nì

GRAMMAR FOCUS

Sentence pattern	Example

Sentence pattern

Example

1. "把" + 趋向补语

我 把 菜 谱 带 来 了。
wǒ bǎ cài pǔ dài lái le

2. "先……然后……再……"

你 应 该 先 找 到 一 个 菜
nǐ yīnggāi xiānzhǎodào yí gè cài
谱, 然 后 把 需 要 的 原 料
pǔ rán hòu bǎ xū yào de yuán liào
买 来, 再 把 它 们 洗 干 净。
mǎi lái zài bǎ tā men xǐ gān jìng

3. "谁" 表示任指

谁 说 问 题 不 大?
shéi shuō wèn tí bú dà

4. 反问句

谁 说 问 题 不 大?
shéi shuō wèn tí bú dà

5. "……没什么"

这 点 儿 小 问 题 没 什 么。
zhè diǎnr xiǎo wèn tí méi shén me

6. 副词 "又"

又 是 红 烧 肉。
yòu shì hóng shāo ròu

7. "一点儿也不" + 形容词

一 点 儿 也 不 腻。
yì diǎnr yě bú nì

8. 助动词 "可以"

吃 红 烧 肉 还 可 以 美 容 呢。
chī hóng shāo ròu hái kě yǐ měi róng ne

9. 语气词 "呢"

可 是 我 还 没 学 会 呢!
kě shì wǒ hái méi xué huì ne

CHINESE CHARACTERS REVIEW

汉字 Chinese character		拼音 *Pinyin*	词语组合 Language composition
简	竹 间	jiǎn	简单　简体字
按	扌 安	àn	按照　按时
教	孝 攵	jiāo	教书　教课
味	口 未	wèi	味道　口味
辣	辛 束	là	辛辣　辣椒
戒	戈 廾	jiè	戒烟　戒备
烟	火 因	yān	抽烟　香烟
院	阝 完	yuàn	院子　医院
呼	口 乎	hū	呼吸　打招呼
容	宀 谷	róng	容易　美容
街	行 圭	jiē	街道　大街
药	艹 约	yào	中药　吃药
婆	波 女	pó	外婆　婆婆

CHINESE CHARACTERS REVIEW

汉字 Chinese character		拼音 *Pinyin*	词语组合 Language composition
腐	府 肉	fǔ	豆腐　腐烂
验	马 金	yàn	化验　检验
饭	饣 反	fàn	吃饭　米饭
减	丶 咸	jiǎn	减肥　减法
安	宀 女	ān	安全　安心
较	车 交	jiào	比较　较量

Unit Six

Environment and Transportation

16 这里的环境太糟糕(zāogāo)了

Getting started

Discuss the environmental and traffic issues of your area. Do you often see notices, such as these below in your area?

A Notice Warning: No Traffic on This Road

请注意：前方修路(qiánfāng xiūlù)，每天下午 8 点到第二天早晨 7 点，这条路禁止通行(jìnzhǐ tōngxíng)，请走 23 号公路(23 hào gōnglù)。

Attention: Road ahead is under repair. 8 p.m. – 7 a.m. all traffic is forbidden. Please take Road No. 23.

Text 1

Ma Ming has arrived at Jack's home.

马明：你好，杰克。

杰克：马明，你好，请进！

马明：你们房间外的垃圾怎么没收走？你看，桶里的垃圾这么满！

杰克：是啊，我也很奇怪 (qíguài)，这些垃圾已经放了两个星期了，清洁工 (qīngjiégōng) 没来清理 (qīnglǐ)。

马明：为什么是这样？

杰克：这也是我要问的问题。你看，我正在给市长 (shìzhǎng) 写信呢。

马明：对，应该把这个情况告诉市长。

Text 2

A letter to the mayor from Jack.

市长先生：

　　您好！

　　我叫杰克，我是一个中学生。我对您的工作有一些失望(shīwàng)，甚至可以说不满意。我们这里的环境太糟糕了。我住在约克街和81街的十字路口附近(fùjìn)。这里的路很宽(kuān)，可是交通(jiāotōng)一直很拥挤 (yōngjǐ)，每天都有很多车通过(tōngguò)。因为这里离市中心比较近，所以路上的行人(xíngrén) 也非常多。但是这里的垃圾已经两个星期没有清理了，污染(wūrǎn) 了我们的环境，大家对这些都很不满意。您是一个受人尊敬(zūnjìng)的市长，我希望您马上解决(jiějué)这里的问题。谢谢！

杰克

2014 年 5 月 8 日

New words

1. 糟糕	zāogāo	*adj.*	terrible
2. 奇怪	qíguài	*adj.*	strange
3. 清洁工	qīngjiégōng	*n.*	cleaner
4. 清理	qīnglǐ	*v.*	to clean (up)
5. 市长	shìzhǎng	*n.*	mayor
6. 失望	shīwàng	*adj.*	disappointment
7. 附近	fùjìn	*n.*	nearby; neighboring
8. 宽	kuān	*adj.*	wide

9. 交通	jiāotōng	*n.*	traffic
10. 拥挤	yōngjǐ	*adj.*	heavy; crowded
11. 通过	tōngguò	*v.*	to pass
12. 行人	xíngrén	*n.*	pedestrian
13. 污染	wūrǎn	*v.*	to pollute
14. 尊敬	zūnjìng	*adj.*	respectable; venerable
15. 解决	jiějué	*v.*	to solve

Notes

1. "你看，桶里的垃圾这么满！"

   你看 is a parenthesis, which means an element is inserted in the middle of a sentence to play an emphasizing role and to draw the attention of the listener.

   毫无疑问，他肯定知道了。

   看来，我们已经迟到了。

   There are many parentheses in Chinese. We'll explain them later.

2. "……甚至可以说不满意。"

   The conjunction 甚至 is used in this sentence to emphasize an outstanding event or a further degree.

   在广大农村，甚至在偏远的山区，都已经看上了电视。

   不但大人，甚至连小孩子也明白这个道理。

3. "这里离市中心比较近。"

   The verb 离 in this sentence shows distance between places, and it can be followed by a location noun to serve as an object.

   天津离北京很近。

   这里离学校只有一千米。

183

Exercise

On your own

1. Rearrange the following words and phrases according to the texts and then write their numbers in the pheonix's tail to make a complete sentence.

(1) 给①　　　正在②　　　　写信③　　　我④　　　市长⑤　　　　呢⑥

(2) 对①　　　您的工作②　　　满意③　　　我④　　　不⑤

(3) 了①　　　已经②　　　　垃圾③　　　放了④　　　两个星期⑤

2. Complete the following sentences using 甚至.

(1) 他工作很忙，常常晚上12点才睡觉，有时_____。

(2) 为了准备考试，他从早到晚看书，_____。

Conversation practice

Finish the conversation first and then practice with your partner.

(1) A：你看，这儿到处都是垃圾，太脏了！

　　B：是啊，真不像话！(So shocking!)

　　A：希望_____！

　　B：_____。

(2) A：_____，有人抽烟，太呛 (to irritate one's nose) 了。

　　B：_____。

　　A：我们去和他说一说。

　　B：_____。

184

Class Activity & communication Task

(1) Work in groups of three classmates. Write an open letter on classmates' opinions about and suggestions to the school, including school environment, logistic service and the amount of homework.

(2) Present your report to the class and give your suggestions.

Reading comprehension

我家离学校不太远，走路20分钟就到了。周围的环境不太好，甚至可以说很糟糕。放学的时候，马路上车多，人也多，所以交通也特别拥挤。

True or False:

① 他家离学校比较近。（　　）

② 他家周围的环境还不错。（　　）

③ 周围的交通一直很拥挤。（　　）

Listen and practice

1. Listening comprehension

(1) Decide whether the following statements are true or false after listening to the recording.

Key words:

上个星期 shàng gè xīngqī (last week)　　发现 fāxiàn (to find / to discover)

这条路 zhè tiáo lù (this road)　　这个星期 zhège xīngqī (this week)

满意 mǎnyì (satisfied)

True or False:

① 杰克家住在约克街和 18 街的十字路口附近。（ F ）

② 杰克家附近的交通很拥挤。（ T ）

③ 这条街的垃圾已经三个星期没人清理了。（ F ）

④ 邻居们建议杰克给市长写封信。（ T ）

(2) Answer the following questions after listening to the recording.

Key words:

李太太 Lǐ tàitai (Mrs. Li)

商店门口 shāngdiàn ménkǒu (on the doorway of the store)

警察 jǐngchá (policeman)　　旁边 pángbiān (side; beside)

心里害怕 xīn li hàipà (to be afraid)　　　　禁止停车 jìnzhǐ tíngchē (no parking)

做错事情 zuòcuò shìqing (to do sth. wrong)

很吃惊地看着 hěn chījīng de kànzhe (to look at ... startledly)

站在这儿 zhàn zài zhèr (to stand here)

Questions:

① 李太太把车停在什么地方？

② 看见警察的时候她为什么害怕？

③ 李太太问警察什么？

④ 警察为什么很吃惊？

⑤ 警察站在李太太的车旁边干什么？

2. **Read the following modern poem.**

假 如 我 当 市 长，
jiǎ rú wǒ dāng shì zhǎng

我 先 盖 无 数 的 楼 房，
wǒ xiān gài wú shù de lóu fáng

让 所 有 的 居 民，用 微 笑 迎 接 太 阳。
ràng suǒ yǒu de jū mín yòng wēi xiào yíng jiē tài yáng

假 如 我 当 市 长，
jiǎ rú wǒ dāng shì zhǎng

我 先 贴 一 张 招 贤 榜，
wǒ xiān tiē yì zhāng zhāo xián bǎng

让 美 丽 的 城 市，不 再 受 到 污 染，
ràng měi lì de chéng shì bú zài shòu dào wū rǎn

让 清 新 的 空 气，充 满 绿 色 的 芳 香。
ràng qīng xīn de kōng qì chōng mǎn lù sè de fāngxiāng

假 如 我 当 市 长，……
jiǎ rú wǒ dāng shì zhǎng

> If I were the mayor,
>
> I would have numerous buildings built,
>
> So all the residents could greet the sun with a smile.
>
> If I were the mayor,
>
> I would advertize for people with talents,
>
> So as to keep the beautiful city free from pollution.
>
> And keep the air fresh, always full of green scent.
>
> If I were the mayor...

Chinese characters

Waste disposal. Delete the redundant words in the following passage to make it clear and smooth.

(蓝蓝、篮篮)的天上白云(漂、飘),

(白、百)云下面马儿(跑、袍)。

挥动鞭儿(响、喝)四方,

百(乌、鸟)齐飞翔。

要是有人来(间、问)我,

这是什么(地、他)方?

我就骄傲地告(诉、说)他,

(近、这)是我的(稼、家)乡。

17 喂，您不能在这里停车

Getting started

Do you know these traffic signs? Can you say them in Chinese?

Text 1

In the school parking lot.

杰　　克：喂，您不能在这里停车！

开车人：你说什么？

杰　　克：这是专用 (zhuānyòng) 车位 (chēwèi)，您不能在这里停车！

开车人：可是我有急事 (jíshì)，附近没有别的车位了。

杰　　克：那边还有一个停车场 (tíngchēchǎng)，您可以去那儿。

开车人：那个停车场也没有车位了。我只 (zhǐ) 在这儿停一会儿，好吗？

杰　　克：您最好尽快 (jǐnkuài) 离开，占用 (zhànyòng) 专用车位是不对的。

开车人：好吧，真是没办法 (bànfǎ)！

Text 2

Xiao Zhao's troubles.

小赵(Xiǎo Zhào)的家离公司很远，他每天必须早(zǎo)早地起床坐公共汽车上班。有时候，他起晚了，上班就迟到 (chídào) 了。还有的时候，公共汽车来晚了，他也迟到。老板(lǎobǎn)常常批评他。他觉得，如果有一辆自己的汽车(qìchē)，每天开车上班，就不会迟到了。

上个星期，小赵终于(zhōngyú)买了汽车。他得意(déyì)地对朋友说，现在好了，明天早晨可以多睡一会儿了。可是第一天开车上班，他就碰到(pèngdào)堵车(dǔchē)，迟到了10分钟。接下去的两天，他都因为堵车迟到了，老板非常生气，批评他说："你已经迟到三次了。"

昨天，他开车去买东西，可是找不到停车的车位。他就把车停在专用车位上了，结果警察(jǐngchá)给了他一张罚单(fádān)。小赵现在很烦恼(fánnǎo)，买车到底有没有好处(hǎochù)呢？你能帮帮他吗？

New words

1. 专用	zhuānyòng	*adj.*	(reserved for) special use
2. 车位	chēwèi	*n.*	parking place
3. 急事	jíshì	*n.*	sth. urgent
4. 停车场	tíngchēchǎng	*n.*	parking lot
5. 只	zhǐ	*adv.*	just; only
6. 尽快	jǐnkuài	*adv.*	as quickly as possible
7. 占用	zhànyòng	*v.*	to occupy
8. 办法	bànfǎ	*n.*	measure; means; way
9. 早	zǎo	*adj.*	early
10. 迟到	chídào	*v.*	to be late
11. 老板	lǎobǎn	*n.*	boss
12. 汽车	qìchē	*n.*	car
13. 终于	zhōngyú	*adv.*	finally
14. 得意	déyì	*adj.*	proud; complacent
15. 碰到	pèngdào	*v.*	to run into; to meet
16. 堵车	dǔchē	*v.*	traffic jam
17. 警察	jǐngchá	*n.*	policeman
18. 罚单	fádān	*n.*	fine ticket
19. 烦恼	fánnǎo	*adj.*	vexed; annoyed
20. 好处	hǎochù	*n.*	good; benefit

Proper noun

小赵	Xiǎo Zhào	Xiao Zhao

1. "他每天必须早早地起床坐公共汽车上班。"

The structural particle 地 can appear either before or after an adjective or a verb. 地 works to connect the adverbial and the center word.

他激动地说："太感谢你了！"（Adjective +"地"+ Verb）

小李慢慢地走回教室。（Adjective +"地"+ Verb）

他说不出地高兴。（Verb +"地"+ Adjective）

2. "如果有一辆自己的汽车，每天开车上班，就不会迟到了"。

如果 in this sentence shows supposition, indicating that if the condition mentioned in the first sentence is realized, then the condition in the following sentence can be realized. The adverb 就 shows a continuation of the previous context and a conclusion reached.

如果你不去，就看不到她的演出了。

Sentences as such can also be valid without 如果 in supposing a certain condition:

你参观的城市越多，学到的历史知识就越多。

3. "你已经迟到三次了。"

三次 in this sentence shows the times of 迟到 and serves as the complement of the entire sentence. The verbal quantifier 次 shows the quantity of the action. Other verbal quantifiers are 回, 遍 and 下。

请你再说一遍。

他去过两回了。

时钟敲了三下。

Exercise

On your own

1. Matching.

(1) 如果你通过了考试，   第二天就会没有精神。

(2) 如果晚上十一点以后才睡觉，   就不能参加考试了。

(3) 如果迟到30分钟，   你就可以去中国学习。

2. Complete the following sentences using structural particle 地.

(1)

你应该＿＿＿＿＿＿＿。(认真)

(2)

你可以＿＿＿＿＿＿＿。(慢)

(3)

明天有考试，你最好＿＿＿＿＿＿＿。(早)

Conversation practice

Complete the conversation. Think of more situations. Practice using verbal phrases with your partner.

(1) A：你去过中国多少次？

　　B：＿＿＿＿＿＿＿＿＿＿＿＿＿＿＿。

(2) A：这个城市你来过几回？

　　B：＿＿＿＿＿＿＿＿＿＿＿＿＿＿＿。

(3) A：这本书你读过几遍？

　　B：＿＿＿＿＿＿＿＿＿＿＿＿＿＿＿。

Class activity & communication task

Which do you think is better, driving a car or taking a bus? Divide the class into two rival debate groups. Decide on a specific topic related to green commuting, and environmental protection. Organize a debate contest where, for example, one group supports driving while the other group supports taking a bus.

我喜欢坐公共汽车，公共汽车比较安全。

我认为还是开车方便些，不用等公共汽车，自由一点儿。

停车位太难找了，我希望大家都坐公共汽车。

我觉得要想保护环境，应该少开车，多坐公共汽车。

要想发展经济，还是应该鼓励大家开车。

Read and talk

滥竽充数

(làn yú chōngshù, Pass oneself off as one of the players in an ensemble – be there just to make up the number. Used of incompetent people or infe-rior goods)

中国古代(gǔdài, ancient times)有个齐宣王，他喜欢一种乐器(yuèqì, musical instrument)叫竽。他最喜欢听 300 个人一起吹(chuī, to play)竽。有个人不会吹竽，但也和别的人混在一起，假装(jiǎzhuāng, to pretend)吹竽挣钱。后来齐宣王死了，他的儿子不喜欢听很多人一起吹，喜欢听单个人吹。这个不会吹竽的人只好走了。

Questions:

(1) Why can this guy who doesn't know how to play *yu* (ancient wind instrument) perform for Emperor Xuan of the Qi State?

(2) Have you experienced the situation where a post is filled by someone without qualification? Share with the class.

194

Listen and practice

1. Listening comprehension

(1) Decide whether the following statements are true or false after listening to the recording.

Key words:

警察先生 jǐngchá xiānsheng (policeman)

交罚款 jiāo fákuǎn (to pay the fine)

5分钟 wǔ fēnzhōng (5 minutes)

收费停车场 shōufèi tíngchēchǎng (pay parking lot)

True or False:

① 小赵以前坐公共汽车上班。(T)

② 小赵买了汽车以后就不迟到了。(F)

③ 小赵又迟到了，所以老板让他离开。(F)

④ 小赵说，他只停了 5 分钟，所以警察没有给他罚款。(F)

⑤ 小赵把车停在收费停车场了。(   )

(2) Answer the following questions after listening to the recording.

Key words:

家乡 jiāxiāng (hometown)   木瓜 mùguā (Chinese flowering quince)

花钱 huā qián (to spend money)

不好意思 bù hǎoyìsi (sorry; embarrassed)

喂猪 wèi zhū (to feed the pig)

Questions:

① 小赵的老板喜欢什么?

② 小赵为什么送木瓜给老板?

③ 老板看到木瓜说了什么?

④ 如果你是老板，听到小赵的话，你高兴吗? 为什么?

2. Read the following ancient poem.

李　白　乘　舟　将　欲　行，
lǐ　bái　chéng　zhōu　jiāng　yù　xíng

忽　闻　岸　上　踏　歌　声。
hū　wén　àn　shang　tà　gē　shēng

桃　花　潭　水　深　千　尺，
táo　huā　tán　shuǐ　shēn　qiān　chǐ

不　及　汪　伦　送　我　情。
bù　jí　wāng　lún　sòng　wǒ　qíng

（唐·李白《赠汪伦》）

Getting on board an outbound ship, Li Bai suddenly hears singing from the bank. Although the water of Peach Blossom Pond runs deep, it is still no match for the friendly feelings of Wang Lun when he sees me off.

Chinese characters

Write the words with the same character according to the example.

例：车——停车　汽车　车位

到——_____　_____　_____

事——_____　_____　_____

美——_____　_____　_____

Silk Road

Launched by ancient China, the Silk Road was an artery of traffic between China and the West. It started from Chang'an (Xi'an today), passed through desert oasis and ended in Rome. To work with friendly neighbors in fighting against the Huns who were frequent invaders, Emperor Wudi in the Western Han Dynasty sent an official named Zhang Qian to visit the Western Regions twice in 139 BC and 119 BC. It took Zhang Qian over ten years to conclude his visits. His journeys took him to countries and regions such as India, Iran, Syria, Iraq, Rome, as well as to the north of the Caspian Sea and the Aral Sea. Later, countries in South Asia, Central Asia and West Asia often sent delegations to Chang'an. This road therefore became the main passage of commercial exchanges between China and these countries.

Via the Silk Road, China's silk products, four great inventions including the art of paper-making and printing, gun power and compass, as well as iron-making, peaches and tangerines were introduced to the West, while grapes, carrots, cotton, glass-making as well as painting, music and even religion were introduced from the West to China. The Silk Road thus became an important passage between European and Asian countries for material and cultural exchanges.

18 谁破坏了我们的家

Getting started

Introduction: Do you like travelling? Do you think current nature conservation efforts are effective? Why or why not?

Text 1

Travel to China.

杰克： 美华，暑假我想去中国旅游，你觉得我去哪里最好？

美华： 中国好玩儿好看的地方很多，你喜欢什么？想去哪儿参观？

杰克： 我喜欢大自然(dàzìrán)，风景很美，空气也很新鲜。

美华： 那我建议你去湖南的张家界，那里是山区，环境很好，也非常漂亮。

杰克： 那里可以爬山吗？爬山对健康有好处。

美华： 当然可以，那里的山可高了。

杰克： 可以乘飞机去吗？

美华： 张家界有一个非常漂亮的荷花机场(jīchǎng)，每天的航班(hángbān)也很多，交通非常便利。你可以上网看看。

杰克： 太好了，谢谢你！我还得看看有没有打折(dǎzhé)的机票(jīpiào)。

Text 2

A story of peasants and elephants.

在中国南方，有一个美丽(měilì)的地方。除了村庄，那里还生长(shēngzhǎng)着很多植物(zhíwù)，也生活着很多动物，是一个旅游的好地方。每年很多人去参观游玩，那里已经变成了一个旅游景区。

最近那里发生(fāshēng)了这样的事情：农民(nóngmín)辛辛苦苦①(xīnkǔ)种(zhòng)出来的粮食(liángshi)，等到秋天收获(shōuhuò)的时候，已经被(bèi)动物吃光(guāng)了。其中，大象(dàxiàng)的破坏(pòhuài)最厉害。农民提出(tíchū)，希望修改现在的法律(fǎlǜ)，不要禁止他们捕杀(bǔshā)动物。

可是如果大象会说话，它们也许会问："谁先破坏了我们的家？"因为以前这里是它们的家。

---

① 辛辛苦苦：to work laboriously; to take great pains

New words

1. 大自然	dàzìrán	*n.*	nature
2. 机场	jīchǎng	*n.*	airport
3. 航班	hángbān	*n.*	flight
4. 打折	dǎzhé	*v.*	(to give a) discount
5. 机票	jīpiào	*n.*	plane ticket
6. 美丽	měilì	*adj.*	beautiful
7. 生长	shēngzhǎng	*v.*	to grow
8. 植物	zhíwù	*n.*	plant
9. 发生	fāshēng	*v.*	to happen
10. 农民	nóngmín	*n.*	farmer
11. 辛苦	xīnkǔ	*adj.*	strenuous; laborious
12. 种	zhòng (zhǒng)	*v.*	to plant
13. 粮食	liángshi	*n.*	cereals; grain
14. 收获	shōuhuò	*v.* (n)	to harvest
15. 被	bèi	*prep.*	*used in a passive sentence to introduce*
16. 光	guāng	*adj.*	all gone; nothing left
17. 大象	dàxiàng	*n.*	elephant
18. 破坏	pòhuài	*v.*	to destroy
19. 提出	tíchū	*v.*	to put forward
20. 法律	fǎlǜ	*n.*	law
21. 捕杀	bǔshā	*v.*	to catch and kill

Notes

1. "那里的山可高了。"

In this sentence, the adverb 可 shows a tone of emphasis.

他跑得可快了！

这回我可放心了。

2. "（粮食）已经被动物吃光了。"

The preposition 被 is used here to form a sentence showing passive voice, in which the subject 粮食 is the target of the verb 吃, and the 动物 after 被 performs the action of 吃. The structure is as such: "Subject + 被 + Prepositional Object + Verb + ..."

蛋糕被弟弟吃了。

衣服被雨淋湿了。

Exercise

On your own

1. Match the left and right columns according to the text.

    (1) 粮食   把庄稼都踩倒了。

    (2) 法律   禁止随便杀死动物。

    (3) 大象   已经被动物吃光了。

2. Word classification

Classify the following words into 4 categories.

(1) 大象   (2) 张家界   (3) 乌龟   (4) 美术馆   (5) 停车场   (6) 农民   (7) 老板

(8) 警察   (9) 旅游   (10) 市长   (11) 爬山   (12) 清洁工   (13) 狗

Animals	_____	People	_____
Places	_____	Activities	_____

Conversation practice

1. Complete the conversation using 被 in the sentence. Practice with your partner.

    (1) A：那盘饼干呢?

        B：_____。

    (2) A：花瓶怎么坏了?

        B：_____。

(3) A：我的书呢？

　　　B：_____。

2. Complete the sentence using 可. Practice with your partner.

(1) A. 你喜欢吃中国菜吗？

　　　B. _____。

(2) A. 你常常很晚才睡觉吗？

　　　B. _____。

(3) A. 你觉得喝茶怎么样？

　　　B. _____。

(4) A. 我想学习打太极拳，你觉得怎么样？

　　　B. _____。

Class activity & communication task

(1) Work in groups of four to five people. Search online news about environmental pollution, and select a report. Make a PPT using clues such as the reasons of the pollution, the impact on the environment and suggestions on pollution control.

(2) Select your representative and report the news to the class.

Reading comprehension

　　我是一个很喜欢旅游的人，放假的时候，常常约上三四个同学一起外出游玩。我旅行一般是用自己的压岁钱，或者再跟爸爸妈妈要一些。可是，昨天爸爸对我说："你长大了，如果想出去旅游，得靠自己挣旅游费用了。"

True or False:

① "我" 常常跟朋友一起出门旅行。（　　）

② 爸爸的意思是，要是想出去旅游，他会给钱。（　　）

Read and talk

中国人常说"读万卷书，行万里路"(dú wàn juàn shū, xíng wàn lǐ lù, Read ten thousand books, travel ten thousand miles)，因为在旅行中可以学到很多知识。我特别喜欢去郊区旅行，特别是山区，那里离城市远，空气好，爬山对健康有好处。

Questions:

① "我"为什么喜欢到郊区旅游?

② 你喜欢到什么地方旅游，为什么?

Listen and practice

1. Listening comprehension

    (1) Decide whether the following statements are true or false after listening to the recording.

    Key words:

    奇妙 qímiào (wonderful)　　　　　河湾 héwān (river bend)

    锣鼓声 luógǔshēng (sound of gongs and drums)

    圆月 yuányuè (full moon)　　　　　通红 tōnghóng (very red)

    True or false:

    ① 杰克去张家界旅游了。(　　)

    ② "奇妙"就是"奇怪"的意思。(　　)

    ③ 在一个河湾边可以听到像敲锣鼓的声音。(　　)

    ④ 那里的月亮，一到晚上八九点钟就是红色的。(　　)

    (2) Answer the following questions after listening to the recording.

    Key words:

    神话 shénhuà (myth)　　　　炎帝 Yándì (Emperor Yan)　　女娃 nǚwá (Nüwa)

    精卫鸟 jīngwèiniǎo (bird Jingwei)　填平 tiánpíng (to fill up)　　比喻 bǐyù (metaphor)

    艰难险阻 jiānnán xiǎnzǔ (hardships and obstacles)　　坚定不移 jiāndìng bù yí (firmly)

    Questions:

    ① 炎帝的小女儿叫什么?

    ② 她怎么死的?

204

③ 她死后变成了什么？

④ 后来它每天都做什么事情？

⑤ 它为什么要做这样的事情？

2. Read and sing

洪 湖 水，浪 打 浪
hóng hú shuǐ làng dǎ làng

洪 湖 水，浪 打 浪，洪 湖 岸 边 是 家 乡。
hóng hú shuǐ làng dǎ làng hóng hú àn biān shì jiā xiāng

清 早 船 儿 去 撒 网，晚 上 回 来 鱼 满 舱。
qīng zǎo chuán ér qù sǎ wǎng wǎn shang huí lái yú mǎn cāng

四 处 野 鸭 和 菱 藕，秋 收 满 畈 稻 谷 香。
sì chù yě yā hé líng ǒu qiū shōu mǎn fàn dào gǔ xiāng

人 人 都 说 天 堂 美，怎 比 我 洪 湖 鱼 米 乡。
rén rén dōu shuō tiān táng měi zěn bǐ wǒ hóng hú yú mǐ xiāng

Hong Lake, Ripples after Ripples

Hong Lake, ripples after ripples, and its banks are where my hometown is.

Riding the boat to cast the net in the morning,

returning home with a boatful of fish in the evening.

Mallards and water chestnuts are everywhere;

you can smell the scent of paddy of the harvest.

Everyone says the paradise is of paramount beauty,

but how can it be compared with my hometown?

205

洪湖水，浪打浪

（电影《洪湖赤卫队》插曲）

梅少山、张敬安词
梅会召、欧阳谦叔词
张敬安、欧阳谦叔曲

Chinese character

Crossword

The following is a big Sudoku with nine small Sudokus inside. Fill in the characters of 我们要保护绿水青山 in each of the nine small Sudokus, making sure that the characters in each horizontal and vertical row are never repeated.

	我	要	们	青				
保		青						们
护			我		山	水	要	青
要		护					保	
			绿					
	们					要		水
我	青	绿	保		们			山
水						绿		要
			水	护	我	青		

World Cultural Heritages in China

As an ancient civilization with a vast territory, China offered the world many cultural and natural heritages. By the end of 2013, China has contributed 47 world heritages to the List of World Heritages with the approval of UNESCO. Among the 47, there're 33 cultural heritages such as the Great Wall, the Forbidden City, the Mausoleum of the First Qin Emperor, the pits of the Terracotta Warriors and Horses, the Confucius Temple, and the Potala Palace in Tibet. There're also ten natural heritages such as the Wulingyuan Scenic Spot, Jiuzhaigou Scenic Spot and Huanglong Scenic Spot. In addition, there're four natural and cultural heritages including Mount Taishan, Mount Huangshan, and Mount Lushan. The number of China's world heritages ranks the second in the world next only to Italy. The capital Beijing alone boasts six world heritages, making it the city with the largest number of world heritages in the world.

UNIT SUMMARY

FUNCTIONAL USAGE

1. Expressing dissatisfaction

我 们 这 里 的 环 境 太 糟 糕 了。
wǒ men zhè lǐ de huánjìng tài zāo gāo le

我 对 这 里 的 环 境 很 不 满 意。
wǒ duì zhè lǐ de huánjìng hěn bù mǎn yì

2. Communicating that something is not allowed

您 不 能 在 这 里 停 车。
nín bù néng zài zhè lǐ tíng chē

3. Expressing that there is no alternative

真 是 没 办 法!
zhēn shì méi bàn fǎ

4. Request and refusal

我 只 在 这 儿 停 一 会 儿, 好 吗?
wǒ zhǐ zài zhèr tíng yí huìr hǎo ma

占 用 专 用 车 位 是 不 对 的。
zhàn yòng zhuān yòng chē wèi shì bú duì de

5. Proposing a suggestion

应 该 把 这 个 情 况 告 诉 市 长。
yīng gāi bǎ zhè ge qíng kuàng gào su shì zhǎng

我 建 议 你 去 湖 南 的 张 家 界。
wǒ jiàn yì nǐ qù hú nán de zhāng jiā jiè

GRAMMAR FOCUS

Sentence pattern

Example

1. 插入语 "你看"

你看，桶里的垃圾这么满！
nǐ kàn tǒng li de lā jī zhè me mǎn

2. 连词 "甚至"

甚至可以说不满意。
shèn zhì kě yǐ shuō bù mǎn yì

3. 动词 "离"

这里离市中心比较近。
zhè lǐ lí shì zhōng xīn bǐ jiào jìn

4. 结构助词 "地"

他每天必须早早地起床。
tā měi tiān bì xū zǎo zǎo de qǐ chuáng

5. "如果……就……"

如果我有一辆车，上班就
rú guǒ wǒ yǒu yí liàng chē shàng bān jiù
不会迟到了。
bú huì chí dào le

6. 动词+数量词

你已经迟到三次了。
nǐ yǐ jīng chí dào sān cì le

7. 副词 "可"

那里的山可高了。
nà lǐ de shān kě gāo le

8. 被动句

(粮食)已经被动物吃光了。
liáng shi yǐ jīng bèi dòng wù chī guāng le

CHINESE CHARACTERS REVIEW

汉字 Chinese character		拼音 *Pinyin*	词语组合 Language composition
拥	扌 用	yōng	拥挤　拥抱
挤	扌 齐	jǐ	拥挤　挤牙膏
尊	酋 寸	zūn	尊敬　尊崇
敬	苟 攵	jìng	尊敬　敬爱
附	阝 付	fù	附近　附属
碰	石 並	pèng	碰到　碰撞
板	木 反	bǎn	老板　黑板
堵	土 者	dǔ	堵车　拥堵
游	氵 斿	yóu	旅游　游泳
健	亻 建	jiàn	健康　健美
航	舟 亢	háng	航空　航班
博	十 尃	bó	博物馆　博士

CHINESE CHARACTERS REVIEW

汉字 Chinese character		拼音 *Pinyin*	词语组合 Language composition	
热	执 灬	rè	冷热	热闹
植	木 直	zhí	植物	种植
苦	艹 古	kǔ	辛苦	苦恼
获	艹 狄	huò	收获	获得
粮	米 良	liáng	粮食	口粮
律	彳 聿	lù	法律	律师
破	石 皮	pò	破坏	破烂

I Vocabulary

Word	Pinyin	Part of Speech	Translation	Lesson
阿姨	āyí	n.	aunt	10
矮	ǎi	adj.	short (of stature)	1
安排	ānpái	v.	to arrange	9
按照	ànzhào	prep.	according to	13
摆	bǎi	v.	to put; to place; to arrange	10
搬	bān	v.	to move (house)	1
办法	bànfǎ	n.	measure; means; way	17
保密	bǎomì	v.	to keep sth. secret; to maintain secrecy	8
被	bèi	prep.	*used in a passive sentence to introduce*	18
边	biān	n.	side	2
鞭炮	biānpào	n.	firecracker	10
变成	biànchéng	v.	to become	15
表示	biǎoshì	v.	to show; to express	10
捕杀	bǔshā	v.	to catch and kill	18
踩	cǎi	v.	to step on; to trample	3
菜谱	càipǔ	n.	recipe	13
参观	cānguān	v.	to visit	4
餐具	cānjù	n.	tableware	12
叉	chā	n.	fork	12
差点儿	chàdiǎnr	adv.	almost	4
场	chǎng	m.	*used for recreational or sports activities*	5
超市	chāoshì	n.	supermarket	2
吵架	chǎojià	v.	to quarrel	9
车位	chēwèi	n.	parking place	17
成龙	Chéng Lóng		Jackie Chan	6

城市	chéngshì	n.	city	2
吃饭	chīfàn	v.	to eat; to have meals	12
吃惊	chījīng	v.	to be startled; to be shocked; to be amazed	14
迟到	chídào	v.	to be late	17
宠物	chǒngwù	n.	pet	3
出	chū	v.	to exit; to go/come out	3
出门	chūmén	v.	to go out	2
厨房	chúfáng	n.	kitchen	2
川菜	chuāncài		Sichuan Cuisine	12
传统	chuántǒng	n.	tradition	11
春联	chūnlián	n.	couplet for the Spring Festival	11
打折	dǎzhé		(to give a) discount	18
大喊大叫	dà hǎn dà jiào		to shout at the top of one's voice	3
大惊小怪	dàjīng-xiǎoguài		to be surprised or alarmed at sth. quite normal; to make a fuss about nothing	14
大象	dàxiàng	n.	elephant	18
大自然	dàzìrán	n.	nature	18
代	dài	v.	to be on behalf of	2
带	dài	v.	to bring	4
担心	dānxīn	v.	to worry	8
刀	dāo	n.	knife	12
到	dào	v.	used as a verb complement to show the result of an action	3
到……去	dào…qù		to go to ...	4
倒	dào	v.	to reverse; to turn upside down	11
得	de	pt.	used to link a verb or an adjective to a complement which describes the manner or degree	1
得意	déyì	adj.	proud of oneself; complacent	17

灯笼	dēnglong	n.	lantern	10
第……次	dì...cì		the ... time (第 used before numerals to form ordinal numbers)	6
点(菜)	diǎn (cài)	v.	to order (dishes)	12
懂	dǒng	v.	to understand	5
读	dú	v.	to read	9
堵车	dǔchē	n.	traffic jam	17
蹲	dūn	v.	to squat	3
朵	duǒ	m.	*used for flowers, clouds, etc*	10
躲	duǒ	v.	to hide	8
儿子	érzi	n.	son	1
而且	érqiě	conj.	and that; in addition	9
耳机	ěrjī	n.	headphones	7
发生	fāshēng	v.	to happen	18
罚单	fádān	n.	fine ticket	17
法国	Fǎguó		France	12
法律	fǎlù	n.	law	18
烦	fán	adj.	vexed; annoyed; irritated	7
烦恼	fánnǎo	adj.	vexed; annoyed	17
方法	fāngfǎ	n.	method	15
方块	fāngkuài	n.	square piece	13
房间	fángjiān	n.	room	3
放(鞭炮)	fàng (biānpào)	v.	to set off (firecrackers)	10
放心	fàngxīn	v.	to set one's mind at rest; to rest assured	5
放学	fàngxué	v.	(school) to let out; (of classes) to be over	7
肺	fèi	n.	lung	14
福	fú	n.	blessing; happiness; good luck	11
父母	fùmǔ	n.	parents	9
附近	fùjìn	n.	nearby; neighboring	16

钢琴	gāngqín	*n.*	piano	6
高	gāo	*adj.*	tall	1
个子	gèzi	*n.*	stature	4
各种各样	gèzhǒng gèyàng		various; all kinds of	5
各自	gèzì	*pron.*	separately; on one's own	2
公司	gōngsī		company; firm	9
宫保鸡丁	gōngbǎo jīdīng	*n.*	spicy diced chicken with peanuts; kungpao chicken	15
恭喜	gōngxǐ	*v.*	to congratulate	10
古诗	gǔshī	*n.*	ancient poem	9
鼓掌	gǔzhǎng	*v.*	to applaud	6
挂	guà	*v.*	to hang	10
关	guān	*v.*	to shut	3
光	guāng	*adj.*	all gone; nothing left	18
锅	guō	*n.*	pot; wok	13
国际	guójì	*n.*	internation	9
过节	guòjié	*v.*	to celebrate a festival	11
过夜	guòyè	*v.*	to sleep over; to put up for the night	8
过	guo	*pt.*	*used after a verb or an adjective to indicate a past action or state*	12
孩子	háizi	*n.*	child	9
汉字	Hànzì	*n.*	Chinese character	9
行人	xíngrén	*n.*	pedestrian	16
杭州	Hángzhōu		Hangzhou	4
航班	hángbān	*n.*	flight	18
好处	hǎochù	*n.*	good; benefit	17
好久	hǎojiǔ	*adj.*	long time	1
盒子	hézi	*n.*	box	3
红烧肉	hóngshāoròu		pork braised in brown sauce	15
呼吸	hūxī	*v.*	to breathe	14

花儿	huār	*n.*	flower	10
化验	huàyàn	*v.*	to test; to examine	14
黄果树瀑布	Huángguǒshù Pùbù		the Huangguoshu Waterfall	4
机场	jīchǎng	*n.*	airport	18
机会	jīhuì	*n.*	chance; opportunity	9
机票	jīpiào	*n.*	plane ticket	18
极	jí	*adv.*	extremely; to the greatest extent; exceedingly	6
急事	jíshì	*n.*	sth. urgent	17
几	jǐ	*approx. num.*	a few; several; some	7
计算机	jìsuànjī	*n.*	computer	9
记得	jìde	*v.*	to remember	4
继承	jìchéng	*v.*	to carry on; to inherit	9
寄	jì	*v.*	to mail; to post	11
夹	jiā	*v.*	to pick up; to press from both sides	12
家	jiā	*m.*	*used for families or emterprises*	10
简单	jiǎndān	*adj.*	simple	13
见	jiàn	*v.*	to see	1
健康	jiànkāng	*adj.*	healthy	9
讲(故事)	jiǎng (gùshi)		to tell (a story)	11
交通	jiāotōng	*n.*	traffic	16
郊外	jiāowài	*n.*	suburbs; outskirts	14
教	jiāo	*v.*	to teach	13
脚	jiǎo	*n.*	foot	10
接	jiē	*v.*	to meet (sb); to pick sb up	8
结果	jiéguǒ	*n.*	result	14
解决	jiějué	*v.*	to solve	16
戒	jiè	*v.*	to give up; to drop; to stop	14
尽快	jǐnkuài	*adv.*	as quickly as possible	17
进	jìn	*v.*	to enter	4

京剧	jīngjù	n.	Peking opera	5
警察	jǐngchá	n.	policeman	17
酒	jiǔ	n.	alcoholic drink	14
开朗	kāilǎng	adj.	sanguine; always cheerful	11
开玩笑	kāi wánxiào		to play/make a joke	11
开张	kāizhāng	v.	to open for business	10
可爱	kě'ài	adj.	cute; lovely	1
客厅	kètīng	n.	living room	2
空气	kōngqì	n.	air	14
夸	kuā	v.	to praise; to compliment	10
筷子	kuàizi	n.	chopstick	12
宽	kuān	adj.	wide	16
困	kùn	adj.	sleepy	6
拉 (琴)	lā (qín)	v.	to play (certain musical instruments, such as violin, accordion)	6
蜡烛	làzhú	n.	candle	10
辣	là	adj.	chilli; hot	13
懒	lǎn	adj.	lazy	7
老	lǎo	prefix.	*used before the noun, adjective, numeral*	8
累	lèi	adj.	tired	6
离开	líkāi	v.	to leave	7
李	Lǐ		Li	1
李小龙	Lǐ Xiǎolóng		Bruce Lee	6
里面	lǐmiàn	n.	inside	3
理解	lǐjiě	v.	to understand	7
鲤鱼	lǐyú	n.	carp	15
例如	lìrú	v.	for example; for instance	9
脸	liǎn	n.	face	1
脸谱	liǎnpǔ	n.	types of facial makeup in Peking operas	5

《梁祝》	Liángzhù		*Butterfly Lovers*	6
粮食	liángshi	*n.*	cereals; grain	18
了解	liǎojiě	*v.*	to understand; to know	8
另外	lìngwài	*n.*	in addition; besides	10
楼上	lóu shang		upstairs	2
楼下	lóu xià		downstairs	2
麻婆豆腐	mápó dòufu		pockmarked grandma's tofu	13
马路	mǎlù	*n.*	road; street	2
卖	mài	*v.*	to sell	2
贸易	màoyì	*n.*	trade	9
没	méi	*adv.*	have not; do not	4
没关系	méi guānxi		it doesn't matter	13
每年	měi nián		each year	11
美好	měihǎo	*adj.*	beautiful; fine	11
美华	Měihuá		Meihua	1
美丽	měilì	*adj.*	beautiful	18
美容	měiróng	*v.*	to improve one's looks	15
美云	Měiyún		Meiyun	1
门口	ménkǒu	*n.*	doorway	3
名牌	míngpái	*n.*	prestigious/famous brand	9
名胜古迹	míngshèng gǔjì		scenic spots and historic sites	4
明星	míngxīng	*n.*	star (a famous performer)	6
墨西哥	Mòxīgē		Mexico	12
哪些	nǎxiē	*pron.*	which (ones); who; what	4
那边	nàbiān	*pron.*	that side; there	10
那天	nàtiān		on that day	10
奶油	nǎiyóu	*n.*	cream	15
男孩儿	nánháir	*n.*	boy	9
南辕北辙	nányuán-běizhé		try to go south by driving the chariot north-act in a way that defeats one's purpose	15
尼亚加拉瀑布	Níyàjiālā Pùbù		Niagara Falls	4

腻	nì	*adj.*	oily; greasy	15
年轻人	niánqīng rén	*n.*	young people	5
农民	nóngmín	*n.*	farmer	18
女儿	nǚ'ér	*n.*	daughter	1
女孩儿	nǚháir	*n.*	girl	1
欧洲	ōuzhōu		Europe	12
胖	pàng	*adj.*	fat	1
胖子	pàngzi	*n.*	fat person	15
碰到	pèngdào	*v.*	to run into; to meet	17
批评	pīpíng	*v.*	to criticize	7
破坏	pòhuài	*v.*	to destroy	18
瀑布	pùbù	*n.*	waterfall	4
奇怪	qíguài	*adj.*	strange	16
汽车	qìchē	*n.*	car	17
前天	qiántiān	*n.*	the day before yesterday	4
墙	qiáng	*n.*	wall	10
巧克力	qiǎokèlì	*n.*	chocolate	15
切	qiē	*v.*	to cut; to chop	13
秦始皇兵马俑	Qínshǐhuáng Bīngmǎyǒng		terracotta warriors and horses in the tomb of Emperor Qinshihuang	4
清洁工	qīngjiégōng	*n.*	cleaner	16
清理	qīnglǐ	*v.*	to clean (up)	16
庆祝	qìngzhù	*n.*	celebration	10
求	qiú	*v.*	to plead; to beg; to request	8
人口	rénkǒu	*n.*	population	2
人们	rénmen	*n.*	people	11
认为	rènwéi	*v.*	to think	14
色、香、味	sè, xiāng, wèi		color, smell and flavor	13
商店	shāngdiàn	*n.*	shop; store	2
上 (个)	shàng (ge)	*n.*	last; most recent	6
上(大学)	shàng (dàxué)	*v.*	to go (to university)	9

上班	shàngbān	*v.*	to go to work	2
上海	Shànghǎi		Shanghai	4
上街	shàngjiē	*v.*	to go shopping	15
少	shǎo	*adj.*	little; few; less	6
身上	shēnshang	*n.*	on one's body	10
生活	shēnghuó	*v.*	to live	9
生气	shēngqì	*v.*	to get angry	7
生长	shēngzhǎng	*v.*	to grow	18
失望	shīwàng	*adj.*	disappointment	16
使用	shǐyòng	*v.*	to use	12
世界	shìjiè	*n.*	world	12
市长	shìzhǎng	*n.*	mayor	16
事情	shìqing	*n.*	thing; matter; business; affair	7
事业	shìyè	*n.*	career	9
收获	shōuhuò	*v.*	to harvest	18
售票处	shòupiàochù	*n.*	ticket office	5
摔跤	shuāijiāo	*v.*	to tumble; to trip and fall	3
帅	shuài	*adj.*	handsome	4
睡	shuì	*v.*	to sleep	6
睡懒觉	shuì lǎnjiào		to sleep in; to get up late	
苏州	Sūzhōu		Suzhou	4
酸	suān	*adj.*	sour	13
虽然……但是……	suīrán... dànshì...		although; but	5
随便	suíbiàn	*v.*	to do at one's will	9
它们	tāmen	*pron.*	they; them (referring to things or animals)	13
太太	tàitai	*n.*	Mrs	1
态度	tàidù	*n.*	attitude	7
提出	tíchū	*v.*	to put forward	18
体检	tǐjiǎn	*n.*	physical examination	14
贴	tiē	*v.*	to paste; to stick; to glue	11
听话	tīnghuà	*adj.*	obedient; heed what an elder	8

			or superior says	
听说	tīngshuō	*v.*	(I) heard (that)	5
停车场	tíngchēchǎng	*n.*	parking lot	17
通过	tōngguò	*v.*	to pass	16
退票	tuìpiào	*v.*	to return ticket	5
万事如意	wànshì rúyì		everything goes as you wish	2
网友	wǎngyǒu	*n.*	net friends	9
往往	wǎngwǎng	*adv.*	often	9
望子成龙	wàngzǐ-chénglóng		wish one's kid a great success in life	9
卫生	wèishēng	*adj.*	good for health; hygienic	12
味道	wèidao	*n.*	flavor; taste	13
问	wèn	*v.*	to ask	3
问好	wènhǎo	*v.*	to send one's regards to	2
卧室	wòshì	*n.*	bedroom	2
乌龟	wūguī	*n.*	tortoise	3
污染	wūrǎn	*v.*	to pollute	16
武打	wǔdǎ	*n.*	acrobatic fighting in Chinese opera or dance	5
武打片	wǔdǎpiàn	*n.*	kung fu movie	6
西安	Xī'ān		Xi'an	4
西方	xīfāng	*n.*	west	10
习惯	xíguàn	*n./v.*	habit/to be used to	2
喜事	xǐshì	*n.*	joyful event	10
羡慕	xiànmù	*v.*	to envy; to admire	4
香港	Xiānggǎng		Hong Kong	1
香味	xiāngwèi	*n.*	delicious / fragrant scent	13
响	xiǎng	*v.*	to bang; to make a sound	10
消息	xiāoxi	*n.*	news	4
小吃店	xiǎochīdiàn	*n.*	snack bar	2
小梅	Xiǎoméi		Xiaomei	2
小明	Xiǎomíng		Xiaoming	7
小时	xiǎoshí	*n.*	hour	6

小提琴	xiǎotíqín	*n.*	violin	6
小心	xiǎoxīn	*v.*	to mind; to watch out; to be careful	3
小赵	xiǎozhào		Xiaozhao	17
笑眯眯	xiàomīmī	*adj.*	smiling	1
写	xiě	*v.*	to write	6
心脏	xīnzàng	*n.*	heart	14
辛苦	xīnkǔ	*adj.*	strenuous; laborious	18
新郎	xīnláng	*n.*	bridegroom	10
新娘	xīnniáng	*n.*	bride	10
新闻	xīnwén	*n.*	news	2
新鲜	xīnxiān	*adj.*	fresh	14
星期天	xīngqītiān	*n.*	Sunday	7
幸福	xìngfú	*adj.*	happy	9
性格	xìnggé	*n.*	personality	11
修	xiū	*v.*	to repair; to fix	7
许多	xǔduō	*adj.*	a lot; a great deal	4
学习	xuéxí	*v.*	to study	7
血	xiě	*n.*	blood	14
烟	yān	*n.*	cigarette; pipe tobacco or smoke	14
严重	yánzhòng	*adj.*	serious	14
眼睛	yǎnjing	*n.*	eye	1
眼镜	yǎnjìng	*n.*	glasses	1
演	yǎn	*v.*	to play; to perform; to act	6
演奏	yǎnzòu	*v.*	to play (a musical instrument)	6
养	yǎng	*v.*	to raise; to keep (as a pet)	3
要求	yāoqiú	*v.*	to ask; to demand; to request	8
咬	yǎo	*v.*	to bite	3
一……就……	yī...jiù...		no sooner than...; as soon as...; the minute...	2
一边……一边……	yìbiān... yìbiān...		as... (used to join two parallel actions)	2

一定	yídìng	*adv.*	certainly; surely; definitely	3
一会儿	yíhuìr		a little while (later);	5
			in a minute	
医院	yīyuàn	*n.*	hospital	14
意思	yìsi	*n.*	meaning	11
饮食	yǐnshí	*n.*	diet	12
鹦鹉	yīngwǔ	*n.*	parrot	3
拥挤	yōngjǐ	*adj.*	heavy; crowded	16
有名	yǒumíng	*adj.*	well-known; famous	15
有时候	yǒu shíhou		sometimes	3
有些	yǒuxiē	*pron.*	some; a few	8
又	yòu	*adv.*	again	2
鱼	yú	*n.*	fish	13
鱼香肉丝	yúxiāng ròusī		fish-flavored shredded pork	13
原料	yuánliào	*n.*	raw material; ingredient	13
圆	yuán	*adj.*	round; chubby	1
院子	yuànzi	*n.*	courtyard	2
(乐) 曲	(yuè) qǔ	*n.*	tune; musical composition	6
糟糕	zāogāo	*adj.*	terrible	16
早	zǎo	*adj.*	early	17
早餐	zǎocān	*n.*	breakfast	2
怎么办	zěnme bàn		how (to do)	5
怎样	zěnyàng	*pron.*	how	15
占用	zhànyòng	*v.*	to occupy	17
这边	zhèbiān	*pron.*	this side; here; this way	10
这样 (吧)	zhèyàng (ba)	*pron.*	like this; so; this way	8
着	zhe	*pt.*	*added to a verb or an adjective*	1
			to indicate a continued action	
			or state	
植物	zhíwù	*n.*	plant	18
只	zhǐ	*adv.*	just; only	17
纸条	zhǐtiáo	*n.*	scroll	11

中间	zhōngjiān	*n.*	middle	12
中药	zhōngyào	*n.*	Chinese medicine	15
终于	zhōngyú	*adv.*	finally	17
种	zhòng	*v.*	to plant	18
重视	zhòngshì	*v.*	to attach importance to; to pay attention to	13
重要	zhòngyào	*adj.*	important	11
周末	zhōumò	*n.*	weekend	6
逐渐	zhújiàn	*adv.*	gradually	5
祝贺	zhùhè	*v.*	to congratulate	11
祝愿	zhùyuàn	*n.*	wish	11
抓	zhuā	*v.*	to take hold with fingers; to clutch	12
专业	zhuānyè	*n.*	major	9
专用	zhuānyòng	*adj.*	(reserved for) special use	17
准备	zhǔnbèi	*v.*	to prepare	11
自相矛盾	zìxiāng-máodùn		to contradict oneself	15
走	zǒu	*v.*	to leave; to go/take away	7
尊敬	zūnjìng	*adj.*	respectable; venerable	16
昨天	zuótiān	*n.*	yesterday	6
作料	zuòliao	*n.*	condiments; seasonings	13
作文	zuòwén	*n.*	composition	6
作业	zuòyè	*n.*	homework	7
坐	zuò	*v.*	to sit	12

(共363个)

II Supplementary Vocabulary

Word	*Pinyin*	Translation	Lesson
现房出租	xiànfáng chūzū	for rent	1
两层楼房	liǎng céng lóufáng	two-story house	1
院子	yuànzi	yard	1
车库	chēkù	garage	1
蜘蛛	zhīzhū	spider	3
刺猬	cìwei	hedgehog	3
乌鸦	wūyā	crow	3
狗	gǒu	dog	3
狐狸	húli	fox	3
画眉鸟	huàméi niǎo	thrush	3
老虎	lǎohǔ	tiger	3
麻雀	máquè	sparrow	3
鹰	yīng	hawk	3
猫	māo	cat	3
狮子	shīzi	lion	3
狼	láng	wolf	3
鱼	yú	fish	3
蛇	shé	snake	3
寻找	xúnzhǎo	look for	3
主人	zhǔrén	owner	3
小猫	xiǎomāo	kitten	3
爪子	zhuǎzi	paw	3
丢	diū	to lose	3
张大夫	Zhāng dàifu	Dr. Zhang	7
哈佛大学毕业	Hāfó Dàxué bìyè	to have graduated from Harvard University	7
专门研究	zhuānmén yánjiū	specialized study	7
青少年	qīngshàonián	teenager	7

父母	fùmǔ	parent	7
心理咨询	xīnlǐ zīxún	psychological consultation	7
"囍屋"婚庆公司广告	"xǐwū" hūnqìng gōngsī guǎnggào	Bridal Chamber Wedding Planners	10
化妆	huàzhuāng	to make up	10
举行	jǔxíng	to held	10
婚礼	hūnlǐ	wedding	10
拍摄	pāishè	to take a picture	10
漂亮	piàoliang	pretty	10
红色	hóngsè	red	10
白色	báisè	white	10
穿	chuān	to wear	10
旗袍	qípáo	cheongsam	10
皮鞋	píxié	leather shoes	10
花儿	huār	flower	10
戴	dài	to wear	10
恭贺新禧	gōnghè xīnxǐ	Happy New Year!	11
祝你在新的一年里万事如意	zhù nǐ zài xīn de yì nián li wàn shì rúyì	May all your wishes come true in the next year!	11
感恩节快乐	gǎn'ēnjié kuàilè	Happy Thanksgiving!	11
圣诞快乐	Shèngdàn kuàilè	Merry Christmas!	11
新年快乐	xīnnián kuàilè	Happy New Year!	11
凉菜	liángcài	cold dishes	12
熏鱼	xūnyú	smoked fish	12
拌海带丝	bàn hǎidàisī	kelp salad	12
白斩鸡	báizhǎnjī	chicken salad	12
热菜	rècài	hot dishes	12
素菜	sùcài	vegetables	12
蚝油生菜	háoyóu shēngcài	lettuce stir-fried with oyster sauce	12
炒扁豆	chǎo biǎndòu	stir-fried hyacinth beans	12

麻婆豆腐	mápó dòufu	pockmarked grandma's tofu	12
荤菜	hūncài	meat	12
松鼠桂鱼	sōngshǔ guìyú	squirrel sweet and sour cod	12
烤鸭	kǎoyā	roast duck	12
京酱肉丝	jīngjiàng ròusī	shredded pork cooked in soy sauce	12
汤	tāng	soup	12
鸡蛋汤	jīdàn tāng	egg soup	12
酸辣汤	suānlà tāng	hot and sour soup	12
三鲜汤	sānxiān tāng	soup with three delicacies	12
主食	zhǔshí	staple food	12
米饭	mǐfàn	rice	12
饺子	jiǎozi	dumplings	12
包子	bāozi	steamed stuffed bun	12
馒头	mántou	steamed bread	12
饮料	yǐnliào	soft drink	12
葡萄酒	pútao jiǔ	grape wine	12
香蕉丽人	xiāngjiāo lìrén	banana split	12
柠檬汁	níngméng zhī	electric lemonade	12
奶油汤	nǎiyóu tāng	cream soup	12
磨菇汤	mógu tāng	mushroom soup	12
洋葱汤	yángcōng tāng	onion soup	12
沙拉	shālā	salad	12
蔬菜沙拉	shūcài shālā	green salad	12
水果沙拉	shuǐguǒ shālā	fruit salad	12
海鸥沙拉	hǎi'ōu shālā	cobb salad	12
热菜	rècài	main course	12
意大利肉酱面	Yìdàlì ròujiàngmiàn	spaghetti	12
酥炸鱼柳	sū zhá yúliǔ	crispy fried fish	12
炸牛排	zhá niúpái	fried steaks	12
甜点	tiándiǎn	desserts	12
水果布丁	shuǐguǒ bùdīng	fruit pudding	12

巧克力圣代	qiǎokèlì shèngdài	chocolate sundae	12
香草冰激凌	xiāngcǎo bīngjīlíng	vanilla icecream	12
前方修路	qiánfāng xiūlù	road repairing ahead	16
禁止通行	jìnzhǐ tōngxíng	all traffic is prohibited	16
23号公路	23 hào gōnglù	Route 23	16

（共91个）

III Chinese Characters

Characters		Pinyin	Lesson	Characters		Pinyin	Lesson
阿	阿	ā	10	传	傳	chuán	11
矮	矮	ǎi ✓	1	单	單	dān	13
按	按	àn	13	刀	刀	dāo	12
摆	擺	bǎi	10	倒	倒	dào	11
搬	搬	bān ✓	1	道	道	dào	13
办	辦	bàn ✓	5	灯	燈	dēng	10
备	備	bèi	11	丁	丁	dīng	15
被	被	bèi	18	懂	懂	dǒng ✓	5
边	邊	biān ✓	2	读	讀	dú	9
鞭	鞭	biān	10	堵	堵	dǔ	17
表	表	biǎo	10	蹲	蹲	dūn ✓	4
兵	兵	bīng ✓	4	盾	盾	dùn	15
捕	捕	bǔ	18	朵	朵	duǒ	10
布	布	bù ✓	4	躲	躲	duǒ	8
踩	踩	cǎi ✓	4	而	而	ér	9
叉	叉	chā	12	耳	耳	ěr	7
差	差	chà ✓	4	罚	罰	fá	17
超	超	chāo ✓	2	烦	煩	fán	7
吵	吵	chǎo	9	方	方	fāng	10
成	成	chéng ✓	6	房	房	fáng ✓	2
承	承	chéng	9	肺	肺	fèi	14
迟	遲	chí	17	福	福	fú	9
宠	寵	chǒng ✓	3	父	父	fù	9
厨	廚	chú ✓	2	附	附	fù	16
处	處	chù ✓	5	钢	鋼	gāng ✓	6
川	川	chuān	12	港	港	gǎng ✓	1

230

格	格	gé	11	夹	夾	jiā	12
各	各	gè ✓	2	架	架	jià	9
宫	宮	gōng	15	简	簡	jiǎn	13
恭	恭	gōng	10	健	健	jiàn	9
鼓	鼓	gǔ ✓	6	渐	漸	jiàn ✓	5
挂	掛	guà	10	讲	講	jiǎng	11
怪	怪	guài	14	跤	跤	jiāo ✓	4
观	觀	guān ✓	4	脚	腳	jiǎo	10
惯	慣	guàn	12	洁	潔	jié	16
龟	龜	guī ✓	3	解	解	jiě	7
锅	鍋	guō	13	戒	戒	jiè	14
孩	孩	hái ✓	1	界	界	jiè	12
喊	喊	hǎn ✓	3	尽	盡	jǐn	17
杭	杭	háng ✓	4	惊	驚	jīng	14
航	航	háng	18	晴	睛	jīng ✓	1
呼	呼	hū	14	警	警	jǐng	17
华	華	huá ✓	1	敬	敬	jìng	16
坏	壞	huài	18	久	久	jiǔ ✓	1
皇	皇	huáng ✓	4	酒	酒	jiǔ	14
获	獲	huò	18	剧	劇	jù ✓	5
机	機	jī	7	康	康	kāng	9
极	極	jí ✓	6	空	空	kōng	14
急	急	jí	17	苦	苦	kǔ	18
己	己	jǐ	8	夸	誇	kuā	10
挤	擠	jǐ	16	块	塊	kuài	13
际	際	jì	9	筷	筷	kuài	12
迹	跡	jì ✓	4	困	困	kùn ✓	6
继	繼	jì	9	蜡	蠟	là	10
寄	寄	jì	11	辣	辣	là	13

懒	懶	lǎn	7	农	農	nóng	18
郎	郎	láng	10	女	女	nǚ ✓	1
累	累	lèi ✓	6	胖	胖	pàng ✓	1
鲤	鯉	lǐ	15	炮	炮	pào	10
力	力	lì	15	碰	碰	pèng	17
例	例	lì	9	批	批	pī	7
联	聯	lián	11	评	評	píng	7
脸	臉	liǎn ✓	1	婆	婆	pó	13
梁	梁	liáng ✓	6	瀑	瀑	pù ✓	4
粮	糧	liáng	18	奇	奇	qí	16
了	了	liǎo	8	墙	牆	qiáng	10
另	另	lìng	10	巧	巧	qiǎo	15
笼	籠	lóng	10	切	切	qiē	13
楼	樓	lóu ✓	2	且	且	qiě	9
麻	麻	má	13	秦	秦	qín ✓	4
卖	賣	mài ✓	2	琴	琴	qín ✓	6
矛	矛	máo	15	轻	輕	qīng ✓	5
贸	貿	mào	9	庆	慶	qìng	10
梅	梅	méi ✓	2	求	求	qiú	8
门	門	mén ✓	2	曲	曲	qǔ ✓	6
眯	眯	mī ✓	1	染	染	rǎn	16
密	密	mì	8	容	容	róng	15
末	末	mò ✓	6	肉	肉	ròu	13
母	母	mǔ	9	杀	殺	shā	18
慕	慕	mù ✓	4	商	商	shāng ✓	2
恼	惱	nǎo	17	烧	燒	shāo	15
尼	尼	ní ✓	4	胜	勝	shèng ✓	4
腻	膩	nì	15	失	失	shī	16
娘	娘	niáng	10	诗	詩	shī	9

使	使	shǐ	12	习	習	xí	7
示	示	shì	10	鲜	鮮	xiān	14
世	世	shì	12	羡	羨	xiàn	4
市	市	shì	2	相	相	xiāng	15
摔	摔	shuāi	4	象	象	xiàng	18
帅	帥	shuài	4	消	消	xiāo	4
司	司	sī	9	笑	笑	xiào	1
丝	絲	sī	13	写	寫	xiě	6
苏	蘇	sū	4	血	血	xiě	14
酸	酸	suān	13	辛	辛	xīn	18
虽	雖	suī	5	幸	幸	xìng	9
随	隨	suí	9	性	性	xìng	11
它	它	tā	13	许	許	xǔ	4
太	太	tài	1	严	嚴	yán	14
态	態	tài	7	眼	眼	yǎn	1
贴	貼	tiē	11	演	演	yǎn	6
厅	廳	tīng	2	验	驗	yàn	14
停	停	tíng	17	养	養	yǎng	3
统	統	tǒng	11	业	業	yè	7
退	退	tuì	5	姨	姨	yí	10
万	萬	wàn	2	易	易	yì	9
往	往	wǎng	9	鹦	鸚	yīng	3
位	位	wèi	17	拥	擁	yōng	16
味	味	wèi	13	俑	俑	yǒng	4
闻	聞	wén	2	于	於	yú	17
卧	臥	wò	2	鱼	魚	yú	13
乌	烏	wū	3	原	原	yuán	13
污	汙	wū	16	圆	圓	yuán	1
鹉	鵡	wǔ	3	辕	轅	yuán	15

院	院	yuàn	2		重	重	zhòng	11
愿	願	yuàn	11		州	州	zhōu	4
糟	糟	zāo	16		逐	逐	zhú	5
占	占	zhàn	17		烛	燭	zhú	10
掌	掌	zhǎng	6		抓	抓	zhuā	12
赵	趙	zhào	17		专	專	zhuān	9
折	折	zhé	18		准	准	zhǔn	11
辙	轍	zhé	15		走	走	zǒu	7
着	著	zhe	1		奏	奏	zòu	6
植	植	zhí	18		尊	尊	zūn	16
纸	紙	zhǐ	11		坐	坐	zuò	12
终	終	zhōng	17					

（共250字）